Woman
in
Motion

By Marlene Adrian

Illustrated by Eliane Mauerberg–deCastro

Women of Diversity Productions, Inc.

Women of Diversity Productions

421 Sandy Lane, Ft. Worth, TX 76120-1717
voice (817) 451-6615 fax (817) 451-5879
internet: dvrsty@aol.com

1996

Cover Design: The Art Emporium, Milwaukee, Wisconsin
Editor: Anne K. Klinger
Layout & Design: Kris Coates
Creative Consultant: Debra F. Campbell
Illustrator: Eliane Mauerberg-deCastro

Printed in the United States of America

10   9   8   7   6   5   4   3   2   1

Address all business and subscriptions to the following:
Fay Klein
400 Antique Bay Street
Las Vegas, NV 89128
voice (702) 341-9807 fax (702) 341-9828
internet: dvrsty@aol.com

Library of Congress Cataloging-in-Publication Data

Adrian, Marlene, 1933–
        Woman in motion/by Marlene Adrian;
    illustrated by Eliane Mauerberg-deCastro.
                p.   cm.
            ISBN 1-884724-04-3.—ISBN 1-884724-03-5 (soft)
            1. Physical education for women. 2. Movement education.
        3. Movement , Psychology of.   I. Title
        GV439.A38   1996   95-50086
        796' .0194–dc20   CIP

Dedication

This book is dedicated to Sue Click and Sherry Pegg of Indianapolis for their encouragement and support.

Preface

This book was written to provide a woman-centered, personalized approach to the enhancement of your life. I hope that the humor and uniquenesses of this book will bring new vitality and exciting concepts to you.

Movement is the essence of being. You move to learn, to play, to survive, and to become one with your body. Fitness, health, and well-being are improved when utilizing this women-centered movement integrated approach. There are many guidelines presented so that you can learn to know yourself as an integrated person and accept yourself as the unique woman you are. The eleven chapters are designed as an enjoyable journey into yourself, your environment, and finding yourself through movement and becoming the woman you want to be.

Development of your ability to move and enjoy your body can have a positive effect upon your self-awareness and self-acceptance. Movement also affects your attitudes, emotions, and feelings. Thus, movement is the bridge to an integrated self. Erase dichotomous and normative thinking, and become the unique woman you love.

marlene adrian

Table of Contents

Chapter One
Enjoy Your Unique Body

We come in all sizes and shapes, and in varying degrees of firmness. Like clouds in the sky, we come in many colors: white billowy clouds, black-gray nimbus clouds, orange streaks across the sky, silvery horse-tails, or pink haze at twilight. Each has a unique beauty. So too, as women, our uniqueness is also beautiful. This beauty is reflected in the diversity of our bodies—their sizes, shapes, and energies. We are endowed with an amount of melanin that determines the color of our skin at any given moment, since the amount of melanin can change during our lifetime. Differences are often linked to nicknames ascribed to us. Nicknames, however, also have been used to hurt those who are perceived as different. But we, as women, can define our bodies in the ways that are understandable and desirable.

We are as diverse and unique as snowflakes and should feel the joy of being so!

*P*erceptions are
relative; maintain
your uniqueness
since everyone may
see you differently.

This diversity is multicomplex, with respect to how we see ourselves and how others see us. And that is what makes for an interesting world! What a bore it would be to be surrounded by clones. I wouldn't find it interesting to see everyone as a replica of myself. Some friends have said that I look Scandinavian, but my ancestry is German. Some think I am too thin, whereas, others think I'm athletic and strong-looking. Some find me old and others say my body is "too young" to be the 62 years it is.

People do not interpret what they see in the same way. Everything is relative—our perception of ourselves and the perception of our bodies by others; our perception today and in a particular situation, and that of tomorrow or in a different situation. For example, I usually consider myself as being extremely tall; and, to a short person, I am perceived as such. But when I am in a room inhabited by women volleyball and basketball elite athletes, I feel short. It is a whole different sensation and perception.

A tall person is a
tall person is a tall
person—or is she?

Live the diversity concept

Diversity means uniqueness, not merely difference. With an acceptance of uniqueness comes an acceptance of value and purpose. Each body has abilities and complements other bodies. I certainly enjoy having my shorter friends help me find things in the crawl space of my attic, or help with other small area tasks. Conversely, they like it when I can put in a light bulb in a ceiling fixture while standing on an ordinary chair. If I want to dance Country Western, it is fun to have one person taller than the other in order to twirl, but then, again, it's fun doing the "tush push" with someone the same height. Many times I have found it relaxing and comforting to lean on a friend with some extra padding, rather than a bony shoulder like mine. Lean, muscular and angular bodies may be sought in time of danger, but large, compliant, curved- shaped bodies are great for cuddling purposes. When each of us has a body different from each other, we have the opportunity to share, to collaborate, to work together and to enjoy together. The short, agile woman basketball player is able to move quickly between the bodies of the taller players. The taller player can get the rebound that misses the basket more easily and will pass it to the shorter player racing to the scoring basket. Diversity is a challenge for us to capitalize upon differences and develop more fully from diverse experiences and interaction. Diversity is beautiful and should not be used as a means of ostracizing or belittling others. Variety truly is the spice of life, and we need to share and enjoy our diversity, since it can be mutually beneficial.

Diversity is beautiful

Did you ever stop to think that those (in TV ads, for example) "promoting" the ideal body may be endeavoring to control you? They may try to prevent you from getting privileges; may keep you in a constrained, inferior role, may prevent you from developing your unique talents, or make you want to be like them because you accept their perceptions of what is ideal? I remember a professor of computer science/electrical engineering who was less than five feet tall, but walked and moved with such assurance that you felt she was a giant and possibly royalty. She became a person "with power" in a predominantly male-dominated field. She definitely did not fit the "ideal body of TV commercials."

It certainly makes for an interesting photograph to see different sizes, shapes and colors of people on the same picture. When we see a picture of "all the same," we tend to think of the individuals as "having all the same" abilities. We tend to stereotype persons. When we see people of diverse sizes, shapes, and colors we are apt to think more of uniqueness—differences. Although some outward appearances do link with some abilities, there is more to an individual than outward appearances. The outward shell can be "dressed" in many ways to bring forth the unique talents of the individual. What is inside is equally important; exterior diversity is intertwined with interior diversity. The two, however, can not be separated.

If we cannot accept different body types, how can we hope to accept different ethnic groups?

Let us delight in the world of uniqueness of each individual—those special attributes that provide intellectual stimulation, interesting conversations, beautiful social interactions and unique physical encounters. Consequently, we must delight in ourselves first. We must come to believe that who and what we are is acceptable and to be loved.

Basic activities to be at ease with your body

First thing in the morning—in bed

Don't crawl out of bed half awake and not sure if you want to get out of bed. Feel your body by wiggling your toes, moving your fingers, stretching your legs, and then reaching upward with your arms as though your hands could touch the ceiling. Next curl as tightly as you can. Follow this with stretching as far as possible with legs, arms, and trunk. Raise your feet and legs above your hips and pretend you are pedaling an inverted bicycle. Now lower your legs and shake your body, everywhere. Move your fingers as though you were playing a piano, using a computer keyboard, or knitting, sewing, or whatever you wish to imagine. Repeat this sequence of actions several times before getting out of bed.

To accept and love ourselves, we must learn to love our bodies.

Stand in front of a mirror

What do you see? A tired face and body; an energetic face and body; an O.K. energy level, or what else do you see? Look at yourself and lovingly accept each part of your body as it is— not wishing it to be different. Make faces at the mirror—smile, frown, smirk, laugh, droop, move your mouth to one side. Repeat and note how your "mirror self" changes, both in posture and energy, as you shape your face. Be aware that your facial expression, and your inner feelings, are radiated to your posture and, possibly, perception of your self.

Stand tall

Now, looking into the mirror, deliberately stand as tall as possible—reach with the top of your head toward the ceiling. Flatten your

abdomen and tuck in your buttocks as you try to ascend into the sky. remember to keep breathing, exhaling and inhaling. Reach with your spine, being careful not to raise or tense your shoulders. Let your arms dangle at the sides of your trunk. Now relax and see how your body changes. Did you maintain almost the same extended appearance or does your body appear to sag,droop, or crumble? Repeat this "stand tall" 3-15 times depending upon how great the discrepancy is between your natural stance and the "stand tall" posture. The greater the discrepancy, the greater the number of repetitions you should perform.

Ready for walking?

Walk from one room to another and listen to your walk, feel your balance, and think of the walking movement. Most persons do not glide gracefully, efficiently, or with a balanced-feeling. There often is a thudding sound when the heel strikes the ground or an unevenness, jerkiness, and asymmetrical sensation as we walk. In addition, the inner feelings, attitudes and thoughts often are transmitted to the walking movement and posture. So learn to walk as a dancer, as a beautifully tuned-energy system, and as the fog silently moving across the land. Whatever metaphor you choose, it should represent flow, rhythm, efficiency and beauty to you. It's your choice.

Be aware
of your
posture.

To experience the joy of walking, stand tall as you did in front of the mirror and lean forward from the ankles until you are forced to take a step to prevent falling. Take 5, 6, 7 or more steps which are naturally caused by the force of the lean, and then gradually stop your movement.

This force is gravity trying to pull you to the ground and you are counteracting with steps to keep your feet under your balance point of your body (center of body weight). Let yourself flow, almost run, with the sequence of standing, leaping, and stepping to maintain balance. Repeat until you feel you can continue walking effortlessly forever. Feel the flow of the movement! Some mornings this will flow immediately; other mornings you might need a few trials to renew the sensations.

Now that you have a feel of gliding, floating, and being effortless, let's concentrate on some basic biomechanics of walking. You want to point the feet in the direction of your walk—do not toe-out more than 10 degrees. This angle is very slight. Greater angulation may cause problems at your joints (ankle, knee and hip). Maintain an erect trunk, tucking in the buttocks and keeping the head aligned with the trunk. Inhale and exhale from the abdomen. Allow the arms to swing naturally, balancing the swinging of the legs. Concentrate on placing the heel and rolling along the sole of the foot until you push with the toes as you take one step after another. Practice walking tall and gracefully until it becomes your natural walk.

*W*alk with enjoy-
ment and beauty—
a sense of well-being
and oneness of self.

Now it's time for a shower

In the shower it is time to get to know your body—caressing it and enjoying its living energy. As you lather your body with soap, feel your body's texture, softness, firmness, lengths, circumferences, and contours. Can you reach all parts of your body? Explore your body and enjoy it—and become aware of all parts and their capabilities. You may analyze or emotionalize this experience. Do both!

Don't forget your breasts. Know what your breast proportions are, how they change in size and firmness and how you feel about them. As you are doing so, conduct a self-examination.

Laminate your self-examination instructions on a card and hang it in your shower. You may also obtain information about laminated shower cards from your local breast cancer clinic, women's resource center, or hospital.

Massage your hands by placing the thumb of one hand in the palm of the other with the fingers on the back of that hand. Stroke the hand 3-10 times moving from the heel of the palm to the fingers. Repeat with the other hand. If your fingers are a bit stiff, reverse the thumb and finger position and stroke with more pressure to stretch and extend the fingers of the other hand. Massage other body parts, such as the forearms, upper arms, thighs, and lower legs. Any kneading-type motion can be used.

Can you reach all parts of your body? What can you do to help yourself reach everywhere? Large sponges, a small towel held at each end, or other devices can be used to "feel" the contour of unreachable body parts. Do you normally stand on one leg to lift the other foot when soaping it and feeling your toes? Is this impossible to do? Why not use a stool in the shower? Or take a bath? You can enjoy your feet and get to know them! Know every day that your body is part of you.

Touch and know your body—it's part of you!

Total movement

Did you know you have more than 256 bones, more than 400 major muscles, and many miles of nerve pathways comprising your movement system? Unfortunately, most persons use only about 20% of their movement capabilities.

Therefore, it is important to know if those bones, muscles, and nerve pathways are still functioning. Although you may not be aware of, or come to know each of these bones, muscles, and nerves, you can learn to use them effectively. Everyday you should strive to activate the total system and check that all functions well.

With the following series of activities, check-out your movement abilities and, through daily practice, keep them functioning. Think of this check as a tune-up, that will take only 3-5 minutes. It's duration is the equivalent of only one musical selection on the radio, TV, cassette, or CD.

If you don't use it, you will certainly lose it!

Begin standing with feet approximately hip-width apart and arms at the side of your trunk. Repeat every action 3-5 times and perform at slow-to-moderate speeds, without causing unnecessary movements of other body parts. For example, when arms are raised, the trunk should remain immobile and extended (no lean, arch, or flexion.)

Shoulders

♦ Lift the shoulders toward your ears and then lower the shoulders. You can lift both together or alternate.

♦ Circle the shoulders clockwise, then counterclockwise.

Arms

♦ Raise arms sideways until overhead and lower.

♦ Raise arms forward until overhead and lower.

♦ Raise arms backward as far as possible and lower.

◆Rotate arms from a palms-in to a palms-out position, moving from the shoulder joint.

◆ Rotate forearms, moving at elbow joint

◆Flex and extend forearms (similar to action of eating, but emphasize extension).

Hands

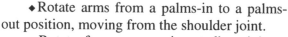

◆ Flex and extend the hands (stretch the fingers and palms as far as possible and move the hand toward the back of forearm for extension; curl the fingers and hand and move hand toward front of forearm for flexion. Again, emphasize extension by performing more of this action than of flexion) .

◆ Move hands in circles, then side-to-side.

◆ Shake-out the arms (shake, shake, shake).

Head

◆Tilt the head side-center-side to try to touch the ear to the shoulder.

◆Stretch the neck upward and then move the head forward and backward, next flex and extend it, and then turn the head right, center, and left, always keeping the neck stretched upward.

The trunk (upper back and lower back)

◆Move your feet to a wider stance and flex your trunk to the right as far as possible, and then to the left—(you may raise one arm overhead to facilitate the stretch to the opposite side).

◆Rotate the pelvis (hip region) making large slow twisting movements.

◆Slightly flexing the legs, flex the trunk forward and backward.

◆Now flex one vertebra at a time beginning with the neck until your trunk is hanging like a rag doll or limp spaghetti. Wait a second or two and then begin to extend one vertebra at a time beginning with the lowest one. The final group of vertebrae to extend will be in the neck.

Legs and feet

For the following exercises choose one of these positions: 1) stand on one leg and balance self, 2) stand on one leg and use a wall for a hand support, 3) sit in a chair, or 4) sit on the floor.

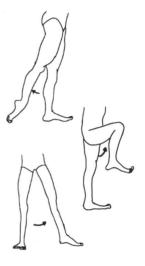

♦ Swing one leg forward and backward slowly and as far as possible.

♦ Raise one leg laterally, and lower.

♦ Raise one leg diagonally, and lower.

♦ Rotate one leg inward and outward with leg extended, then with leg flexed at the knee.

♦ Flex the lower leg to try to touch the foot to your buttocks and then lower and lift the knee to the chest.

♦ Circle the foot, move it side-to-side, flex and extend it (up and down).

♦ Repeat above with other leg

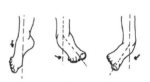

Total body

♦ Shake the body, every part.

♦ Walk in place; swing arms in a circle— counter- and clockwise, single and both arms.

♦ Think of the many movements you can perform and do so.

Enjoy your body; its shape, size, firmness, and movement capabilities, knowing that diversity is valuable. If we change, it should not be for change's sake, nor for conformity, but to love what we become. Remember that change can occur to some extent, but we all inherit chromosomes from our parents, and since we've no voice in choosing who they are, we start with a foundation that might not have been what we would consider "preferable." But on this foundation we can build and remodel; albeit there are limits. We will discover how to love all these aspects as we explore our bodies.

Think of continuums and circles

Another major rethinking, beyond diversity as beautiful, is to stop thinking in dichotomies. There is no either/or, yes/no, this/that, big/little, right/wrong, black/white category with only two choices, except those that humans fabricate. We must not place ourselves, or our bodies into compartments that cannot change or are clearly one or the other—always opposites. Everything should be viewed as a continuum or a circle. The continuum concept means that there are varying degrees of everything. Day doesn't miraculously become night, or night become day. There is dawn and dusk, there is bright white, dull white, duller; light gray, grayer; charcoal black, blacker, with each blending from one to the other without a clear bifurcation or delineation. In the continuum, night continues through the same blending of colors as it circles into day. There is no dichotomy, but a continuous circle of variations.

Similarly, a person is not tall or short, but is measured on a scale—a continuum. Likewise, obesity is measured in amounts, and bodies can and should be viewed on a continuum or a circle with respect to varying percentages of fat in the body. Contrary to what many "experts" state, a woman does not become overweight on the basis of a numerical value. For example, it is ludicrous to think that a person would be declared "not overweight" at 25.9%, but "overweight" at 26%. Such thinking is as ill-founded as declaring a person old at age 50 years, but not old at 49 years and three hundred sixty four days. Rarely do instant transformations take place within us, or between us.

Even mathematicians reject binary logic in favor of "fuzzy logic" and reality—there are infinite possible values between zero and one.

Dichotomies are stereotypes of things, people, and characteristics of people. Society often puts a value judgment on the stereotype, with one being "good" and the other "bad," or "moral" and "immoral." Such judgments are relative to the times and the persons making them. Thus, women considered voluptuous and desirable by men of the Renaissance era are considered obese by today's romance and health writers.

A circle becomes a line and a line becomes a circle.

Nothing is what it appears to be, even gender. Biologists write of the two sexes (genders) male and female. But did you know that some frogs and fish can change their gender, some animals are bi-gender, and human beings also have been classified in different societies as being other than a two-gendered species? All embryos are female with female brains. Differentiation occurs later. Some babies are born with dual reproductive organs, and the delivering medical personnel make the decision as to which organs to keep and which to eliminate. Throughout history, eunuchs, hermaphrodites, and androgynous people have existed. Even, within the male-female dichotomy, the levels of estrogen and testosterone vary. Some men appear to have breasts. Some women are as muscular, or more so, than male weight lifters. Older women may show growth of a beard or mustache and older men may become more woman-like. Thus, gender may be viewed as a circle with maleness and femaleness blending and separating along the perimeter. Chromosomal differences exist, but many other attributes vary within each gender, as much as between genders.

*P*eople have
always desired
absolutes, but there
are exceptions to
every rule. Living
things are complex;
it is time to enjoy
this and erase
dichotomies.

The average or mean of a group of women may be 5 ft. 5 in., with respect to height. Using the "normal probability curve" approximately 68% will be more than 2 inches greater or shorter (one standard deviation from the mean) than this height. There will be women taller than 6 ft. 2 in. and shorter than 4 ft. 10 in. The mean for a group of men will be taller than that of the women but more than 68% of men and women will be clustered together. It is only the extremes that appear to be separated. Thus, homogeneity between the sexes may be as great as within one sex.

With respect to an obesity probability curve, the norm is denoted as the mean, but no one knows the precise variance from that mean representing the change between a normal and an abnormal amount of fat. In addition, most measurements of body fat are merely estimates. Depending upon the measuring tool, this estimate may be 10-30% in error. To complicate the evaluation further is the fact that the amount of fat will fluctuate during the day—morning, afternoon, evening, before a meal, after a meal, after a snack, etc.

Let's forget norms, dichotomies and think of ourselves as being the dynamic, living bodies that we are. Constantly changing and modifying our rate and direction of change, we all have our places on the continuum circle of existence.

We are unique!

Appreciate all body types

Scientists have classified body types into three groups, each with a 7 point scale to rate the degree to which each body type exists in an individual. The three body types are defined as:

Ectomorphic– linear, thin
Endomorphic– fat
*Mesomorphic–*muscular

Since no one is solely one of the three body types, the person is given a numerical score on all three, such as 3-5-4, denoting the combined body somatotype. Most persons have ratings of 3-5 on each of the three body types and are considered average. If the person rates a 6-7 on one body type (for example, ectomorphy) and 3 or less on the other two body types, then the person is said to be ectomorphic. We can match the somatotypes as shown in the following illustrations with Twiggy as the Ectomorph and Mama Cass or Ella Fitzgerald as the Endomorph. The Mesomorph is best represented by women bodybuilders, such as Stephanie Van de Weghe. Stephanie is one of the world's strongest women. She bench-pressed 285 pounds, dead-lifted 450 pounds and squatted 485 pounds to become the 1994 champion of World Powerlifting.

Elite athletic performances are linked to body types, but most movements, sports, and physical activities can be performed adequately by persons of any body type. If you want to be an Olympic long distance runner, however, it would be easier to do so as an ***ectomorph.*** You would have more than enough muscle to move your skinny, light-weight body. Less effort would be required to run the long distance than if you were carrying extra fat, and even extra muscle, particularly in the shoulders and arms. If you observe distance running competitions, you'll see that the majority of runners, and probably all the fastest runners, are ectomorphs.

Our parents give us our body types, but we use the environment to fine-tune them.

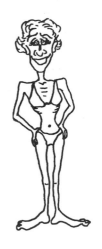

The ***endomorph*** makes one of the best swimmers of the English Channel. Women hold all the records for open water swims. Women with extra fat also are the famous pearl divers of Japan, diving into the freezing waters to bring oyster shells to the surface for tourists and corporations. Since fat weighs less than bone, muscle, and water, a person with extra fat will float in the water easily. If the fat is distributed in the thighs, as with women, they will float horizontally. It is much easier to swim, enjoy the water, and be safe falling from a boat when you have a little extra fat. Another instance in which fat may be helpful is when playing contact sports, such as football, basketball or ice hockey. The fall or collision doesn't hurt if you have a little extra natural padding.

The ***mesomorph*** is the construction worker, chain saw operator, discus/hammer thrower, or farm worker, and is characterized by being strong with pronounced muscles. Physical work requiring lifting heavy loads can be performed easily by mesomorphs. In sports, most female athletes are high in mesomorphy.

Body types are not cast in stone; they can change, and change significantly. It is a case of a continual interaction between genetics and environment—we move and function based upon what we inherit. As we move, we change our bodies because of the way in which we use them.

Know that disproportional bodies exist

Do you know someone who is thin, except in the waist and hip region where abundant fat exists? We are not always proportionally built— the tall person does not always have big feet; conversely, some short persons have huge feet.

Big hands and large bones may exist in a person with relatively small-boned legs and small feet. Muscles may be well-developed in the shoulders and upper trunk and less-developed in other parts of the body. Many women will have more fatty tissue in the lower body than upper body, since women tend to accumulate fat around the hips and upper thighs. The shapes of bodies vary greatly due to genetic disproportionality, developed asymmetries, and specific uses of the body parts. Some women of average height have longer legs than some women who are six feet tall.

Think of all disproportionality as being interesting, commonplace; proportionality is not necessarily the mode.

Understand the relationship between your breasts and self

Are you always going to be a size A, B, C or D? Although we might have done something during our infancy days to affect the size of our breasts, it is unlikely that environment is the primary determinant of breast size. As babies we might have been able to increase our physical activity level and lower our fatty-food intake to prevent enlargement of fat cells, thus moderating breast size. But the disposition to relative breast size has been inherited. Changes in breast size, however, can be influenced by age, diet, pregnancy, activity-level and other factors. We know that many mesomorphic women and athletic women are small-breasted. This may be due to the effect of athletic environment upon the women, but, more than likely, it is due to the fact that large-breasted women self-select themselves out of athletics. Inadequate sports brassieres and inability to reduce pain from sensitive large breasts are probable causes.

It is important for you to look at your breasts and ask yourself how you feel about them. What role do they play in your behavior and love of your body? How do they mesh with your concept of your ***integrated self?***

Do you try to hide your breasts? Have your breasts recently changed with respect to size or shape? Think of your breasts as part of you, an ever-changing dynamic living being. Become aware of how you can free, constrain and otherwise manipulate your breasts in your search for an integrated self and a healthier fitness lifestyle. Large breasts need to be constrained by comfortable means, such as sports/athletic/ fitness bras. Thus, the large breasted woman can find joy in physically active leisure activities. Painful breasts may be a more complex condition to overcome. Changes in nutrition may be a solution, as may "woman's natural medicines". Physical activity may be an influential factor in reducing pain and appearance of breasts.

Understand the relationship between strength and body size

You might think that being tall means being strong, but this is not necessarily so! Many tall women may be able to lift and carry large cumbersome objects because of length of arms, not because of superior strength. The short person often is stronger. Look at all the records in weightlifting—these have all been achieved by short persons. Short arms have better leverage than long arms. If you are short and want to impress that tall friend of yours, go to the health spa and start leg presses and arm presses. You'll soon be able to out-perform your friend. Don't tell her the reason is that for every lift you perform you are not moving the weight as far as she is. Short legs and short arms equal short lifts and less work, but you get credit for the same number of lifts and presses performed by a person lifting the weights a higher distance. Note the strength of the short women gymnasts! Although they have developed muscular strength, their body weight remains less than the average woman's. Their body types also are mesomorphic, developed through intensive training. Despite their potential, however, if short-limbed persons do not exercise their muscles, the advantage in size is lost.

D̲on't stereotype body size with strength.

Understand the relationship between speed and body size

Size alone does not determine speed, but all things being equal in types and amounts of muscle, body length does influence linear speed potential. Long arms and legs have an advantage in producing greater linear speed when throwing a ball or striking a tennis ball, golf ball

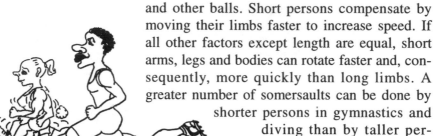

and other balls. Short persons compensate by moving their limbs faster to increase speed. If all other factors except length are equal, short arms, legs and bodies can rotate faster and, consequently, more quickly than long limbs. A greater number of somersaults can be done by shorter persons in gymnastics and diving than by taller persons. When running short distances, size doesn't seem to matter; the faster swinging of the legs of the shorter person neutralizes the longer steps of the taller person and, therefore, both can run at the same speed. The shorter person, however, often can accelerate faster. This may be attributed to the fact that though we inherit fast twitch muscle fibers, we also develop them. Whatever we possess can be modified. We can choose to enjoy the physical activities at which we excel, but we also can enjoy and be capable in most recreational activities.

Speed is influenced by the amount and type of muscle fiber you possess. This is partially inherited, but modifiable by exercise.

Many of us have problems

Misalignment of leg bones, curvature of the spine, malformed feet and generally "poor posture" are anatomically-based problems caused by malnutrition, disease, illness, and generally incorrect habits. These and disuse of muscles and overuse of other muscles also cause common functional postural problems, most of which can be corrected. Chronic problems and disabilities classified as permanent, however, can only be coped with via adaptability techniques. But there are numerous ways to do so— including compensations and uses of external devices, such as a wheel chair. Often the anomaly (commonly referred to as abnormality or disability) interferes with the normal functioning of the "normal or able" body parts.

Consequently, a person compensates by modifying her movement patterns and the way in which she performs activities of daily living and other tasks. This creates greater problems. The integrated self is an interrelationship of all body parts and functional systems. If the problem is functional , not structural or permanent, you can systematically correct your compensation until the anomaly has been eliminated. For permanent problems, adaptability skills can be learned to enhance your strategies for coping with the anomaly.

*W*hatever your problem, there are numerous ways to adapt and capitalize on your attributes.

What is the status of your body? What do you want it to be able to do? Reflect upon these questions as you read the next chapter.

Chapter Two
Develop Your Integrated Self

Healthy means different things to different women. Traditionally, to be healthy was to be free of disease. That definition, however, is too narrow. It is similar to saying that our goal in life is to survive, not to live. To be healthy, we must possess the abilities to enhance the quality of our lives.

It is time that we, as women, define healthy for ourselves—and healthy need not be the same for all women. For example, use the term integrated-fitness instead of healthy. Fitness is an action-word, and denotes a continuum of various degrees of fitness, as well as types of fitness. It is not an either/or situation, i.e., healthy or unhealthy or fit or unfit. Such dichotomous thinking is dangerous and is best avoided. Health, as with fitness, denotes a continuum or a multiple of continuums, since health is multi-faceted.

Integrated-fitness denotes this multi-dimensional aspect of the total you. For example, we may have a very healthy skeleton (bone health), but lack stamina (low cardiovascular health) or locomotor coordination (inadequate muscular/neurological/skeletal health). Locomotion refers to moving from place to place by our own body power, through execution of movements such as walking, running, skipping, and leaping. Thus, health and fitness encompass both structural and functional components; each is important. In addition, there are the psychological, social, and emotional aspects of fitness/health. We can compartmentalize all into the well-known triad of mind, body and spirit, but this fragmentizes the person, and ignores the integrated self. All aspects of the self are interdependent and interrelated. The person responds and behaves as an integrated being, not as a mind, a body, a set of muscles, or an emotion.

Live life, don't just survive.

T͟h͟ink integration!

Health and fitness will be used interchangeably. You may choose either word in your efforts to achieve an integrated self and enhance the quality of your life. You are encouraged to select a word that better defines your goals for you. The most important concept to remember is that you do not "sign up for" someone else's definition of health or fitness or that you do not choose too narrow a perspective. Men within the patriarchal system have consistently determined what was healthy for women and what was healthy for men. The two resulting healthys were not the same. To be fit for bearing children was the only thing considered healthy for women. Men could be healthy for war, and the play of war, that is, sports. Although at times in the past, and for certain classes of women, some sports were considered healthy for women, other sports were still unhealthy or masculine. Fitness, traditionally, meant fit for war. A nation had to become fit to fight, and women fit to bear sons that someday would be soldiers. Even today, despite the trend away from the fitness for war concept, we hear statements from members of the President's council on Fitness to "become fit for your country." It is time to be fit for ourselves. Fitness for women should encompass the integrated concerns and problems of women. Career women often suffer from foot problems due to dressing for the "social (male-desired) image" of the job; that is, wearing high-heeled shoes with toe-squeezing characteristics. Few fitness programs include concern for fitness of our feet.

Y͟our hands and feet need woman-centered fitness.

Women still outnumber men in jobs requiring computer keyboard or typewriter-based activities. Carpal-tunnel syndrome and chronic neck and shoulder pain are problems resulting from these jobs. Fitness for the job requires consideration for the jobs being performed by women.

As a woman, you need to understand the effect of prescribed sex-roles upon your life processes relative to remaining or becoming fit/healthy. For example, outward characteristics of adults are perceived differently for men compared to women. The male is considered to be distinguished and attractive when he acquires a graying of his hair, but a woman has lost her youth and is old and unhealthy when her hair whitens. These statements are based upon the values of a patriarchal society that relate appearance to sex appeal. Women must gain their own sense of the healthy/fit image of self and not be unduly and detrimentally influenced by the male-dominant power in society. Here is a way to do this!

Practice the 3 A's of self-integration

Women-centered fitness is based upon:

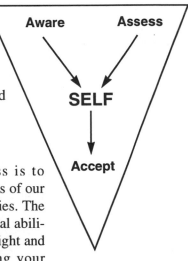

+ self-Awareness
+ self-Assessment
+ self-Acceptance

The 3 A's require internal goals, a uniqueness of fitness relative to self, and a dynamic continuum of becoming.

Self-awareness

The first area of self-awareness is to become aware of the physical dimensions of our bodies. We all have our own unique bodies. The second area is being aware of our physical abilities, such as muscular strength, body weight and coordination. The third area is feeling your body, feeling the tension, the exuberance, the aches, the freedom and just learning to feel something.

Self-assessment

In order to evaluate your fitness you need to know what your definition of fitness is. What is important to and for you? Can you do what you want to physically do? Then evaluate your capabilities according to your needs.

Self-acceptance

Your attitude should be one of lovingly accepting yourself—who you are and what you think you want to be. Only you can control your integration of self; that's what women-centered fitness is. In defining fitness for yourself, it might help to consider these definitions from other women:

*W̲o̲m̲a̲n̲-̲c̲e̲n̲t̲e̲r̲e̲d̲
fitness is being fit
for yourself, your
needs, and your
lifestyle.*

◆ To be fit is to have some energy left after a full day of work.

◆ Healthy, to me, is to not have headaches, aches, or stress.

◆ Fitness is being able to do whatever I want to do—climb the pyramids on a trip to Egypt; play weekend softball; go bicycling with my children; learn to play the piano.

◆ I am fit when I can perform all my activities of daily living, work, and leisure, and have enough vitality to perform extras or respond to emergencies and not be tired the morning after.

◆ I have integrated fitness when I am free to be me and not have constraints preventing me from daring to try whatever I desire.

Self-awareness—definitions that suit you and your lifestyle

What do you perceive as "being fit?" List the characteristics and behaviors you want to possess. You might write such things as—want to be able to walk for 2 hours without getting out-of-breath; want to gain 20 pounds; want to lose 20 pounds; want to fit into those leather pants; want to be able to play racquetball; want to swim 20 minutes; want to have painless feet; want to be happy, etc.

Note the differences of the items in the list with respect to specific wants and general wants. It is very difficult to take action with respect to "to be happy," but very easy to act on "able to walk 2 hours." Separate your list of items into specifics and generals. Hopefully after addressing the specifics, the generals will have been addressed.

Specific Behaviors List (e.g., smile at least 3 times a day)	**General Characteristics List** (e.g., be happy)

Self-assessment-learning how

There are several major ways to conduct a self-appraisal and determine whether or not your lifestyle is one that leads to, or is, the quality of life you desire:

◆ Look in the mirror and give yourself a personalized test.

◆ Test yourself on a "feeling good activity" of your choice.

◆ Organize a set of activities to practice and use as self-appraisal tests.

Look in a mirror

As soon as you rise in the morning, look in a mirror. Do you like what you see? Liking yourself is the best way to health and fitness. Ask

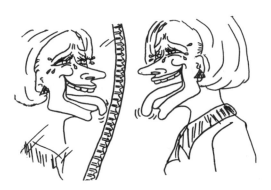

yourself if you are happy to be alive. Are you looking forward to the activities of the day? Do you like your job, lifestyle, responsibilities, and things you do? If all your answers are negative, you would be better off going back to sleep. But one doesn't improve one's joy of life by taking that action. So why not think of one thing you will do today that you look forward to doing, one new person you will encounter, or one thing you will learn today. Begin to anticipate the joy of being alive. Think of yourself in a new light. Start the day by laughing with your mirror image. The facial muscles need to be used—they are as much a part of your body as your hands and feet.

Look in the mirror and laugh with yourself.

Feeling good appraisal

Select one activity that you can test yourself (self-assessment) everyday with respect to "feeling good." For example, when I taught at a university in a small rural town I tested myself on the stairway between the building where I worked and the library. There were 67 steps to climb. I would take the steps two at a time and move at a moderate speed. At the top, I would pause and assess my feelings—was I invigorated? Was I exhausted? Did my legs feel like spaghetti? Did I climb the steps in a record time? If my replies were not favorable, I evaluated possible reasons why not. I usually discovered that I had not had enough sleep, not eaten well that morning, or was stressed out. If such negative reactions occurred I resolved to eat better, get more rest, and relax.

When I moved to flatland Illinois, I needed to change my "feeling good activity." I decided to assess my balance by standing on one foot while putting on one shoe and tying the laces. Then I repeated with the other leg. This was another way I could feel integrated with myself—concentrating on balancing my body and coordinating my fingers to perform a required activity of daily living. Other women told me they did the following to assess themselves on "feeling good:"

Select a "feeling good" activity to practice each day.

♦ Played octaves on the piano as fast as possible to feel good about agility of fingers.

♦ Baked a loaf of bread, evaluating all the movements of kneading the dough to feel good about making something.

♦ Pulled weeds from the flower garden to feel good about being able to reach down and squat.

♦ Walked from chair to chair in her house sitting and getting up at each chair to feel good about moving her large body.

♦ Typed 2 pages to feel good about hands and fingers, brain and cognition.

When the "feeling good activity" doesn't feel good anymore, it is time to think about changing your lifestyle or your "feeling good activity." Find a new hobby or rediscover an old one, read a book, make a new friend, have a conversation with an old one, sit and really absorb your environment, take time to listen to your inner self.

Activities of long duration can also be used to evaluate yourself. If you engage in an aerobics class, music lesson, jam session with the drums, walking program at a shopping mall, weight lifting class, karate or yoga class, etc., you can keep a log of your "feeling good" days and those "less than good" and "pretty poor" days.

Set of self-appraisal activities

Throughout this book you will find activities for becoming a woman in motion. These are described and a testing procedure is given to chart your status. Charts are included as examples of how to keep a log of your progress and construct a profile of yourself. You can try the following activity relative to general movement abilities and use this to check your "feeling good" status.

*A*ssess what
you can do.

Start a timer and perform this sequence as fast as safely possible:

♦ Walk to the kitchen and take a glass, half fill it with water, set it on the counter.

♦ Open a drawer and take a set of flatware and place it on the kitchen or dining room table.

♦ Sit at the table and rise and bring the water glass to the table.

♦ Walk to the living room and turn on the television (or radio or CD or phonograph), sit in a soft chair.

♦ Rise from the chair, turn off the television and return to the timer and stop the timer.

Recording Chart (Log)		
Date	Time to Complete	Comments on Difficulties
_____	_____	_____
_____	_____	_____
_____	_____	_____
_____	_____	_____
_____	_____	_____
_____	_____	_____

Record several trials in one day or one trial every day until you have an average performance. Then test every few days to be sure you have not "fallen behind." Repeat several times a day to improve your performance and practice general movement abilities.

Self-acceptance—know changes are inevitable, but not predictable

Almost all aspects of your life, including biological changes, are reversible or modifiable in someway. If you begin to lose muscular strength, cardiovascular endurance, anaerobic power, bone strength, memory, reaction time, flexibility, speed, energy, or ability to cope with stress, these losses can be counteracted with changes in rest/relaxation, exercise, and nutrition—what I term the REN approach to feeling good. It is true that most changes in women are due to disuse or use, rather than aging or not aging. Although diseases which create losses and dysfunction may not be overcome, negative side effects from the disease usually can be reduced using REN. For example, if you decide not to go walking anymore because you have arthritis, much of the decline in mobility will be a result of the disuse, not the arthritis per se. The important thing is for you to recognize signs of loss—unhealthy events, lack of fitness, inability to perform "feeling good activities" at your usual performance level and do something.

Don't wait until the loss is 30-50%. Be aware of your level of functioning so that you recognize 10% losses. For example, as stress builds during the day, be aware of the initial signs of neck ache and change your activity immediately. You can do some stretching to counteract the movements producing the ache.

Eye stress causes losses in eye function and ability to complete tasks. To alleviate eye stress close your eyes and relax your posture—droop. Then open the eyes and look right, left, upward, downward and forward by moving only the eyes; keeping the head immobile.

Eyes require exercise, too.

Practice REN—relaxation, exercise, nutrition

Relaxation

Relaxation techniques are used to manage, prevent and relieve stress. The "total you" must be involved in such a process. After you have achieved the ability to relax, you will be able to achieve adequate sleeping patterns. Adequate sleep is defined as: you will be able to awaken without an alarm clock and will feel "energized." The next level after relaxation is to achieve serenity through meditation, contemplation, dreaming, or just feeling good about life.

You can close your eyes and fantasize using non-stressful images, such as floating on a cloud, watching beautiful bodies on a beach, or whatever is visually relaxing. When participating in recreational activities such as skating. the brain can relax as the actions become automatic.

Exercise

Exercise can be whatever you select. You can select activities like walking, alternating between sitting and standing, dancing, an aerobics class or just having fun moving. That's what exercise is: moving your body or body parts frequently, intensely, and long enough to make a difference. If you think of long enough as being equivalent to duration or time, you can create acronyms DIF or FIT to remind you of the three prerequisites of effective exercise: duration/intensity/frequency or frequency/intensity/time. There should be no pain, frustrations, depressions, or other adverse sensations. Maybe there will be some aches since parts of your body may have been dormant for years, but no pain.

Exercise a little at a time, at your own pace, with gradual increases in effort until you feel comfortable putting exercise into your daily life. Side-effects should be perspiration, faster heart rate, faster breathing, concentration on your movements, and awareness of what you are achieving.

Think beautiful fantasies and relax.

Exercise should be comfortable and fun for you.

*W*hat is your
exercise style?

Health and fitness are achieved by exercising the integrated self. Sedentary habits, abusive use of your body, and stressing yourself beyond tolerable limits violate exercise guidelines and fitness concepts. On the other hand one can become an exercise fanatic and overdo it, which is also counterproductive.

An adequate exercise program consists of a wide range of movement choices in the following categories.

Flexibility

Use every body part in every way possible—move in all directions, at a variety of speeds, and from a variety of orientations with respect to gravity. We lose flexibility from birth onward, not only when we become middle-aged. We selectively use only some parts of our bodies as we choose the activities and habits of life. Most movements are performed in the anterior/posterior plane, such as when we walk, lift, eat. These are flexion movements and extension as we return to starting positions. Rarely do we move laterally, except in activities, such as dancing and playing sports. Although sports often require more flexibility than daily living tasks, most sports do not require the same amount of flexibility with both right and left arms and legs.

Muscular strength and power

Muscles do not get strengthened if we do not use them. This happens primarily when we move in set or narrowly-defined ways. We forget to use all our muscles in our daily activities. Use every muscle in your body to contract against gravity or other forces, known as resistances, as you move each body part throughout its entire range of motion. Move forcefully, but slowly for strength enhancement. Move quickly against less resistance for power enhancement.

Aerobic capacity

Move continuously with cyclical or other rhythmical movements that elevate the heart rate and increase circulation of blood, air exchange and oxygen take-up for at least 15 minutes. Start with shorter periods interspersed with slow walking until 15 minutes is achieved. Remember to increase the intensity gradually.

Anaerobic capacity

Move rapidly and intensely for short periods of time generating high breathing rates and the necessity to stop. This may be as short as 5 seconds, but try to do 10-20 seconds of high intensity movements followed by a rest period of twice that duration and repeat 3-5 times.

A-B-C's of perceptual-motor ability

Move in response to external cues, objects or persons, such as throwing and catching a ball or playing table tennis. Move your body to develop agility, balance, coordination and sensory enhancement. The latter is often termed perceptual-motor enhancement.

Remember your agility, balance, coordination, and sensory integration.

Body awareness

Be aware of movement and move for the movement, not an external goal, such as scoring more points in basketball. The goal of body awareness is to move and be an integrated self concentrating upon each aspect of the movement. Tai Chi, interpretive dance, yoga, diving, and gymnastics are some activities which increase body awareness and, thus, develop sixth sense (kinesthesia), spirituality, body image, self esteem, and a sense of freedom.

***B**e free to move however and wherever you wish.*

Nutrition

It is important to balance your nutritional program and ingest food when you need it. You need to eat the foods that are necessary for the lifestyle you have or want. Your diet should result in enough energy for you to complete your tasks of the day and have a reservoir of energy for leisure activities. Of primary importance is that you have the energy to move your body when and where you want.

Think of the different body weights you've carried in your lifetime—or were you always the same weight? At which body weight did you feel best? Would you like to recapture that feeling? Don't compare your weight too closely with published charts. Charts are helpful, but body shapes and sizes vary among persons of the same height and body weight. Some women inherit a large-boned frame with short stocky arms and legs. Others inherit a delicate skeleton with long arms, short legs, and big hands. Yes, the environment affects what was inherited, but unless a disease or permanent injury occurs you will be tall if your genes "are for tallness."

Some women are thin, some chubby, some fat, some muscular, but the majority are a mixture of these characteristics and considered average.

The media figure and you— incompatible?

Why is the criterion for the best body the one that is "slender, but with curves in the right places?" Whose criterion is this? Doesn't this reflect the patriarchal view of what is attractive, rather than a healthy/fit female body? Based upon the concept of probability and what we know of body types (refer again to chapter 1 if you wish), less than 15% of women have the healthy potential to resemble the "slender image of fitness" presented to us through the media.

A woman-centered integrated fitness approach means that you decide the best criterion for determining if you have optimum weight and musculature. I would propose that one such criterion might be the ability to move your body. Can you honestly say that you have optimum ability to perform daily tasks with ease? Can you move about without feeling tired or pained carrying your body weight up and down a stairway, walking through a grocery store, or just getting around? If you cannot, then it is time to think of losing or gaining weight, or gaining some muscle. If you think you move optimally, then don't change your body weight. It is right for you.

Unless you are truly unhappy with your physical body, don't try to change it; learn to appreciate it!

In subsequent chapters, basic concepts and applications of REN will be presented. You can then make an informed decision to change or maintain your present self, always in accord with your uniqueness as a woman.

Chapter Three
Create Your Life Spaces

Your life space is the usable or familiar world of your existence. It includes such spaces as your home-space, work-space, play-space, movement-space, cultural-space, person-space and travel-space. Are you spending all your time within the city in which you live, in the neighborhood in which you live? How often do you enter into the travel-space? How diverse a group of people and subcultures do you know? How often do you use your play-space? How large and how frequently visited are all the spaces that comprise your life space?

Each of us occupies space relative to our size, shape, needs, and desires.

It is important to optimize our life space, expanding or retracting it relative to each situation. Expansion of life space is necessary and rewarding when the world appears constricting and routine, when there is a lack of excitement, adventure, creativity, motivation, or zest for living. Many women do not venture from the familiar and predictable. Possibly there is

*L**earn to feel comfortable with, and free to change, your life space.*

a fear of the unknown and an uncertainty for venturing from the comfort of the familiar. But this reduces our opportunities to learn and grow.

Sometimes a woman extends her life space until it consumes her energy and drains her life force because the life-space becomes unmanageable. Often this will occur during holiday seasons, when visitors arrive, and when too many deadlines need to be met. Then the life space may be retracted to allow a person to seclude herself in a supportive cocoon-type space. Gradually, she will then expand the life space, sometimes replacing the stressful spaces with new spaces, such as a new leisure-space. At other times a constraining work-space consumes all the person's life space, without room for personal-space. A career woman, a woman fearful of losing her job, and an artist are persons who often need to expand their personal space because of an all-consuming work-space.

Fundamental to a woman's life space is her body-space. How she uses this space influences her behavior, and conversely the use of body-space is reflective of her sense of personal well-being. Control of our body-space is one step toward control of our life space. Our body-space is our most personal and powerful space. It should be easiest to control since we have the power to integrate our body and mind to move in whatever space we direct ourselves. Because of one reason or another, however, many of us move as if we were in chains, a puppet on strings, surrounded by a space shield only inches from our skin.

We can do something about this situation, and enjoy our body-space and expand and control our environment. The following are some activities to practice to enrich your body-space.

Your body

◆ Sit in a chair and slowly draw your knees to chest and feet to buttocks and flex your trunk and neck to curl into a very, very small ball. Next slowly extend the legs and arms to be as long and wide as possible. Feel the extent of your body!

◆ Repeat these actions while lying in bed or on the sofa or floor.

◆ If you are on a beach, lie on the sand and touch as much sand as you can with your arms and legs to create an expansive form in the sand. Then curl and be only a dent in the sand.

◆ If you are in a swimming pool, lake or calm ocean, you can do the same actions and feel the varying amounts of water resistance against your movements.

Stand and create postures of smallness, largeness, restrained and expansive characteristics. Next, combinations, i.e., the legs expand and the top half of body pulls inward, can be made to challenge the moving of your body parts.

Your space

Stand, with feet parallel and at least hip-width apart, in the center of a room in your residence. Without moving your feet slowly reach with your arms as though you were trying to touch the wall in front of you. Next reach to the right side to try to touch the wall to your right; repeat reaching to the left and behind you. Now try to touch the ceiling. Repeat these actions to each wall and the ceiling, as well as, to the corners of the walls. Move your body as great a distance toward the direction your hands reach, but do not move your feet. Move slowly.

Repeat the previous actions but assume different foot positions: stand with right foot a large step in front of the left, reverse the foot positions, etc.

Now take a step with each reaching arm action. Make the step as long as possible, possibly similar to a lunge. Remember to move slowly and maintain your balance.

Continue to take slow, long steps until you actually reach a wall and can touch it. The goal is to take as few steps as possible in order to reach and touch the wall.

Your body-space

Move through the room, avoiding obstacles and changing your posture to fit the space. Move on/in each obstacle/piece of furniture in the room. If a chair is small, sit using as many different postures and directions possible.

The environment and your life space

Your body-space is the physical part of your life space. Our life space encompasses the environment in which we exist. Within our environment we must consider the people with whom we interact, the tools we use, the buildings in which we work, play and reside and the atmosphere which we breathe. Inclement weather or a prevalence of crime, for example, may curtail our night-life and our life space.

As we learn to appreciate our body and become aware of how we use, or could use, our body-space, we can begin to function more effectively within our environment. There is a tendency for women to respond to the environment, rather than manipulate it. We should guard against being controlled by our environment, which also relates to the people within it. Possibly, being able to control our life space will make it easier to expand and enrich it. Certainly, we will be able to utilize the environment to our benefit. If we always try to adapt to our environment, we will probably experience problems. Moreover, a constant, controlling environment results in repetitive behavior, which results in risk of stress and injury.

Sense and appreciate how much space your body can capture.

Routine is a potential environmental problem

Repetitive behavior often results in what is known as the repetitive trauma syndrome. Chronic aches and pains, mental problems, and stress are symptoms of this syndrome.

Let's look at this repetitive trauma syndrome (RTS). Whenever a movement is repeated over-and-over so that we are "pushed" beyond our level of tolerance, we experience a type of fatigue stress (RTS). For example, if we sit at a desk continuously for two or more hours at a time, several chronic symptoms may occur, such as, swollen feet or ankles, low back ache, painful buttocks, or tight neck and shoulders. Another example is a woman who runs 3 miles every day and feels pain in her knees and back.

Repetitive trauma usually strikes because of work-related activities. Hobbies, however, can result in RTS just as easily.

Standing a long time often results in blood pooling in the legs and feet. Stress to the lower back also occurs. The trunk may become kyphotic (upper trunk flexion, shoulders drawn inward). Pain and varicose veins may result.

What to do?

- Stepping in-place every five minutes.
- Sitting for a few seconds every half hour and raising the feet.
- Periodically standing on one leg, lifting the other leg, and then lowering it; repeating with other leg.
- Periodically standing on one leg, swinging other leg slightly.
- Wriggling your toes frequently.
- Contracting/relaxing lower leg muscles through isometrics.
- During break, sitting with legs above the heart (easily done in the restroom).
- Walking frequently.
- Standing with one foot resting on a stool, cabinet drawer or railing while working.

Sitting many hours a day may result in tight (stressed) shoulder and neck muscles, low back pain, sore buttocks, and occluded blood supply to feet. Sitting produces greater stress on the spinal column, especially at the low back (lumbar) area, than does standing.

What to do?
- Stand and stretch arms overhead and stretch the spine.

◆ Lift your feet frequently.

◆ Reposition yourself every half hour.

◆ Clasp your hands behind your back and pull downward drawing your shoulders down and back.

◆ During break, walk briskly and "tall."

◆ During break, sit with legs above the heart (can easily do this in the restroom).

Using the computer or typewriter may cause eye strain, hand numbness, neck and shoulder tension, and what is known as the carpal tunnel syndrome, which is pain and numbness of the hands and wrists due to one or more of the following: pinched nerve, pinched blood vessel and tendon slippage or impingement at the wrist.

What to do?

◆ Place the hands in the neutral position to perform tasks. In the neutral position, hands are aligned with forearms and not in extreme flexion or extreme extension. This may require changing the level of the keyboard or making a forearm pad.

◆ Every 30 minutes extend your fingers, spread your hands, lift the hands overhead and circle them, lower the hands to your side and shake arms so hands feel like noodles.

◆ Change your eye focus, close your eyes, do eye exercises as shown in chapter 2, page 40 and generally give your eyes a rest every 20 minutes.

◆ Move your documents and other tools so that you can work with a minimum of head tilt and trunk flexion. Place yourself in as erect a position as possible.

Lifting objects during the eight hour work day can create low back pain, shoulder strain, tired legs, hernia, and strains to many muscles if fatigue or twisting occurs.

What to do?

♦ Reach your arms overhead and stretch your spine between lifts.

♦ Use your total body to lift; your legs can help by flexing and extending, by bumping the load with the thigh to a higher position.

♦ Try to vary the ways you lift objects, intervals between lifts, and order of lifting. Intersperse reaching type activities between lifts.

♦ Lift light weights at home or work with a strength trainer.

♦ Avoid twisting your trunk as you lift.

Using a hammer for long periods of time can create trauma of hammer-nail impact to the elbow and wrist. Carpel tunnel syndrome also can occur.

What to do?

♦ Use a curved handled hammer.

♦ Use a hammer with a shock absorption handle

♦ Avoid full extension at the elbow.

♦ Change the positioning of hammering— side swings, downward swings, upward swings.

♦ Loosen the grip at instant of impact; this is easiest to do on downswings.

♦ Shake arm and hand until noodle-like.

Playing musical instruments creates unique problems with the back, hands, and shoulders.

What to do?

◆ Stand during each "resting period" no matter how short.

◆ Adjust the chair to induce an erect trunk with feet supported.

◆ Learn to relax during pauses in playing.

Most sports, especially ball-type sports, produce asymmetrical muscle action and asymmetrical development of the body

What to do?

◆ Engage in total body movements as described in chapters 1, 5 and 8. These are considered warm-up activities but are essential for general body development.

◆ Simulate the sport movement with the other arm and leg, e.g. right-handed tennis players will mimic or play left-handed actions.

◆ Strengthen the non-striking, kicking, throwing side of body with muscle exercises as described in chapter 6.

◆ Play games which utilize both hands. These could be such games as dodgeball, cageball, variation of volleyball using two hand throws instead of striking the ball, non-dominant hand dribbling keep-away. Make up your games!

Many hours of walking, running, jumping and aerobics can cause impact trauma to the feet, legs, hip and lower back. If the impact shock from landing on hard surfaces occurs frequently and above the tolerance limits of the body, pain, strains, sprains and fractures could occur.

What to do?

◆ Buy shoes with super shock absorption materials.

◆ Run and jump on earth paths and fields.

◆ Reduce the frequency of impacts.

◆ Learn to cushion the impact with correct biomechanics techniques, i.e., flex the legs at landing; let your body "give" with the impact.

Guidelines to remember:

◆ Search for tools that fit your body.

◆ Search for chairs and other furniture to fit your body.

◆ Modify the environment with items, such as, foot rests. Then your feet will comfortably rest on a surface.

◆ Modify the environment.

Unless you are average in size and height, our human-made environment doesn't fit us. We are too tall or too short for the chairs, rakes, brooms, vacuum cleaners, counters and table tops, to name a few objects we use.

If you're left-handed—wow! The problems abound. It is no wonder that people say left-handers are creative and intelligent. They have had to cope, adapt to a right-handed world.

Life is an experience of adapting to the environment. Think of the environment as having many solutions and not as being a problem.

Chapter Four

Stop Premature Aging

Aging is a normal process which begins at birth. Premature aging, however, can begin at any age. We see premature aging in many persons: the twenty year old who cannot get into or out of an automobile, climb stairs or walk fast or run; the thirty year old who moves as though all her joints are arthritic, even though they are not; the fifty year old who believes walking is the perfect and only exercise, but cannot play the piano, make bread or throw a softball as she could at 30 years of age; the sixty year old who, afraid of falling, restricts her movement to her room in a retirement home. With all these persons, body functioning has been lost, and they cannot move as they once did. This has not occurred because of illness or disease, but because they have forgotten how to use their entire bodies, usually due to disuse and possibly because they listened to others. Behavior is often governed by other people. What about you? Have you fallen prey to such behavior? Is your answer "yes" to any of the following questions?

◆ Because others expect less of you, do you comply?

◆ Do you think it is no longer appropriate to play or to fantasize—do you think you must ACT YOUR AGE?!?

◆ Have you given in to an injury or disease rather than trying to do as much as you can with the capabilities you have retained?

◆ Have you fallen into a state of disuse?

◆ Are you letting others control your health by imposing their definition of health upon you?

*Use your
integrated body
or you will lose
your abilities
to function.*

In order to prevent premature aging, you need to recognize the process and discover ways to circumvent such disuse-aging. You need to identify types of movements you consistently forget to use and then learn to incorporate them into your lifestyle. Learning to use your body effectively and joyously will result in prevention of premature aging and will enhance the quality of your life.

Movement is you

It is through movement that we are able to change our lives—our self-image, self-confidence, and behavior. Movement is the purest form of what some persons think of as exercise. Exercise has many connotations; it may be separated from the whole person and done for external reasons, such as exercising because it is the fad, exercising because other people say we should, believing that if we don't exercise we will be less acceptable by colleagues and potential friends, or fearing that due to a lack of exercise we will die of a heart attack. Are you one who loves to exercise, are you young and energetic, have you always exercised and played sports—is it part of your lifestyle? Or do you enjoy sports only now and then? Possibly, however, you are a woman who says, "Exercise? I've never exercised in my life, and I don't intend to start now! Furthermore, I don't have time and I have no one with whom to exercise ."

*Through
movement
you can grow
healthier as
you grow older.*

But in reality, you have always exercised, because you have always moved. Movement is more than exercise; it is a way of life. Through movement we can synthesize our body and self and learn to love ourselves. Movement is required for all the activities we do day-in and day-out, as well as night activities. We only can function independently if we move. We move when we eat, write, play softball, mow the lawn, play the guitar, etc. Maintaining our movement skills enables us to expand our life space and learn new things.

Add another dimension to your lifestyle by moving for movement's sake. The essence of movement is what you will seek as you move. Start with the following activities to find the essence of movement.

Movement focus

Stand or sit so that you have room to raise your arms sideways. Start with arms hanging, at your sides. Read the sequences of movements and then perform them with your eyes closed.

♦ Raise your arms to the side to a horizontal position and then lower them again moving at a slow speed, pausing at the raised and lowered positions for one second each.

♦ In your mind see your arms producing the movement and note the "butterfly wing" pattern that your body forms.

♦ Move faster, eliminate the pauses, and see the new pattern—how does it differ? What other sensations do you feel—need for maintaining balance? acceleration? breathing? involvement of body parts other than the arms?

♦ Change the pattern; raise your arms forward pausing at the horizontal and to the overhead position and down. See the movement in your mind. Inhale on the upward movement and exhale on the downward movement.

From the movement produce a visual image in your head.

♦ Repeat the movement at a comfortable rate for you and concentrate on the breathing. Feel a sense of serenity flow through your being.

♦ Move other parts of your body and sense and visualize where movement is in space and the patterns made.

Movement momentum

◆ With your eyes open swing your right arm horizontally from left to right, and return it to the starting position on right side of body. Repeat this action increasing the speed of the swing and the involvement of the rest of the body. For example, add trunk rotations, leg rotations and finally turn the whole body by turning on the right foot and lifting the left foot from the ground.

◆ Repeat the sequence with your left arm.

◆ Feel the momentum lift you from the ground and/or continue the turn for you.

◆ Now try other momentum-producing movements such as swinging a leg, jumping.

Movement tension

◆ In a sitting position, shake your hands and fingers. Feel the lack of tension, the looseness in your hands and fingers.

◆ Extend the hands upwards and lower, repeating with a gradual increase in muscular force of extension without increasing the speed (move slowly). Continue to breath normally or exhale on the extension of the hands and inhale as you return the hands to a neutral position. Feel the force transmitted from tendons in hands to muscles in forearms, and later to your shoulders, neck, and even your face as you attain maximum voluntary tension in your extension movement. Notice that you seem to want to hold your breath, not inhale or exhale—please continue to inhale and exhale.

◆ Gently flex your fingers to make a fist with one hand. Open the hand and make another fist, but use a bit more force. Continue until you

Movement creates other movement.

are using maximum force to create as strong a fist as possible. Note how your body and head tend to change position during the forceful fist.

◆ Repeat with your other hand.

◆ Repeat simultaneously with both hands making fists.

◆ Repeat the tense action with your feet. Move the feet toward the shin bone in what is called dorsi-flexion. Feel the radiation and release of tension throughout the body.

Learn to sense tension of movements and strive to use only the required tension to produce the movement, Let the movement determine the tension, not the tension interfere with your movement.

Tension in one body part will radiate to other body parts, since you are an integrated being.

Movement touch

◆ Sit and close your eyes. Lift both hands in front of your chest palms facing each other and 1-2 inches apart. Move the two little fingers until they touch each other. Move each of the other fingers to touch the corresponding finger of the other hand. Set-up patterns such as same finger touch—1 to 1, 2 to 2, 3 to 3, 4 to 4, 5 to 5 in sequential order and next in random order. For example, use finger touches 1 to 4, 2 to 3, 1 to 5, 3 to 4, etc.

◆ Stand and close your eyes. Use your right hand to touch other parts of your body, such as, left knee, right ankle, left shoulder, top of head. Repeat actions with the left hand.

◆ Open your eyes and touch your right hand with the left as follows: a light stroking, a tap, a slap and a pressure. Repeat with other hand. Do the same sequences with each foot—one foot touching the other foot.

Movement continuity

◆ With your arms, create continuous movement by making curved movements, such as circles, ellipses, figure 8's with each movement leading into the next movement without pausing. Use one arm initially if you wish or start immediately with both arms. Think of your hands as creating a great painting, forming patterns in the air, orchestrating a symphony of movements or whatever else your thoughts envisage. Move with continuous flowing paths for approximately 20 seconds (or until you feel you want to stop).

◆ Now move in linear and angular paths, disrupting the continuity. For example, move the hand forward and stop, reverse direction and return to the starting position. Experiment by moving in different directions and note the staccato, non-flowing, jerky, actions. Move with this non-continuous quality for approximately 20 seconds (or until you feel you want to stop).

◆ Alternate continuous movement for 10 seconds and non-continuous movement for 10 seconds for a total of one minute. For example, move the arm as though tracing figure 8's for 10 seconds. Then simulate the splashing of water. After the minute, think of what you felt, became, or envisioned while you were moving and especially when you changed the movement type. Was there a difference in the quality of movement and sense of self? In what ways?

*D*evelop your kinesthetic sense— become the movement.

It is by practicing all these movement aspects—focus, momentum, tension, touch, and continuity—that we learn to control our movements, and thereby, our ability to function in daily living tasks, work activities, and play. We regulate and govern our movements and develop our sixth sense—*kinesthetic sense*. This is the ability to perceive without the input from any of the other 5 senses. Kinesthesia is our awareness of where our body and body parts are in space, their orientation to the earth, the speed of our movements and the directions of the movements without "seeing them with our eyes." We feel the quality of movement affecting our thoughts, emotions, and feelings. We empower ourselves and can change the movement to be what we want it to be. In so doing, we can feel young, free, unrestricted and shed thoughts of aging.

Repeat all the described movements with your eyes closed and concentrate on the feel of the movement. Develop your kinesthetic sense.

If you are healthy, fit and movement-able, continue with your lifestyle but become more aware of your self—your body, feelings, abilities, and thoughts.

Learning to love yourself can prevent premature aging and recapture the joy of being alive.

Self-appraisal and practice

Self-appraisal is merely a technique to determine the current status of your ability or characteristic. It is not judgmental, but only for your information and use. You evaluate how well you can perform activities and cope with life. With self-appraisal, first you appraise yourself: select a particular aspect such as the ability to climb the stairs to your third floor apartment. Next ask yourself the following questions. Are you satisfied? Is a small amount of change desired? Are you dissatisfied most of the time? Are you dissatisfied only in certain situations you can easily identify; for example, when carrying groceries? Write the answers so that you can refer to them later. You decide, not others. If you are a relatively slow mover, and a friend of yours is a fast mover, avoid comparison of yourself to your friend. To paraphrase Thoreau, "move to your own internal drummer."

Now you are ready to try a self-appraisal test of your movement-fitness. This appraisal refers to how well you are able to move—to perform all those activities you want and/or need to perform. There are no norms, you are the criterion for appraisal of your current status of what is termed movement-fitness. You test yourself, record your score, and construct a profile, a visual picture of your capabilities. This profile will be considered as your baseline profile, since it reflects your status now before any conscious effort to change it. At the end of the chapter are representative profile charts and directions for constructing your baseline profile. Your profile can be used to check your status and reduce the possibility of premature aging sneaking up on you and catching you unaware.

Activities for self-appraisal

The following types of activities have been selected for your self-appraisal: locomotion, changing levels, transferring objects, balancing, eye-hand-ball coordination and manipulation. Not only, do these represent the general classification of all actions normally encountered in life, but they can also be measured.

Use any timer available—a clock or watch with a second hand, an egg timer, a TV clock display, a fitness/sports watch, etc.

In order to measure your performance, the following equipment is needed: charts found in this book, a pencil, a ruler or tape measure, a tennis ball or other small ball, chairs and a timer of some type. Practice with the timer to be sure you know how to start and stop quickly and to read the elapsed time. You will need to practice starting and stopping the timer with either hand since you will need to use the left hand with the timer as you perform right-handed tasks, and use the right hand with the timer as you perform left-handed tasks. You will need to develop accuracy with timing periods as short as 10 seconds.

All the items of the self-appraisal test can be done within a 30 minute period. You may do one a day, or several a day, rather than all of them on the same day. Retest yourself periodically, possibly each two weeks.

Locomotion appraisal

The ability to move from place-to-place is a pre-requisite for expanding your life space and functioning effectively in life. Most of us can walk from place-to-place; some use wheel chairs or other devices or assistance. Walk with your cane, crutches, walker, holding the arm of another person or push your wheelchair. All can take this test.

To accept and love ourselves, we must learn to be at home with our bodies.

Select a space in your house where you can walk in a prescribed route, such as the length of a hallway or the length of two rooms connecting through a doorway, The walking route should be such that you will be walking 20-60 seconds. Place the timer where you can start it as you begin to walk and stop it as you finish the walk. Walk as fast as you safely can.

Locomotion Appraisal

distance walked _____   time to walk _____

Test recording

Repeat this test on the same day and on three or four other days until you achieve scores on at least 10 trials using the same route. Study the scores and select the most typical value. For example, if your times were as follows: 15 sec., 12 sec., 19 sec., 14 sec., 15 sec., 16 sec., 15 sec.,

Walking Record

1_____

2_____

3_____

4_____

5_____

6_____

7_____

8_____

9_____

10_____

sum_____

avg._____

14 sec., 16 sec., 15 sec., your typical value (the mode) is 15 sec. You will record 15 sec. on this test. If the scores do not cluster in a small range, you can calculate an average score (sum of all scores divided by the number of scores). In this example, the sum is 142 and the average time is 14.2 (divide by 10). Thus you can record 14 as your baseline score. This represents your status now, before you begin any thought of changing or prevention of loss in performance.

Variations

Double the distance. Start the timer. Walk the distance, turn, and return to the starting position. Stop the timer. Record your score.

Changing levels

In our daily lives we lie, sit, stand, stoop or squat, and change the level and position of our head. Common activities in which changing levels occurs are when gardening, cleaning hard-to-reach areas of your house and getting in and out of bed, a chair, a canoe, etc. It is important to evaluate our skill in doing these types of activities, since we are apt to avoid doing some of these movements as we become older, and supposedly wiser. Thus, loss of function occurs with us being unaware of such loss. When a situation occurs when we must change levels, we might find that we cannot do so. Then we cannot partake in the joy of the activity.

Assessment and practice changing levels

Sit-stand-walk-turn

Place two chairs side-by-side facing a table or piece of furniture upon which you can place your timer. Have the chairs far enough away from the table for you to comfortably walk between the table and pair of chairs (C1, C2). Place a chair (C3) (kitchen, dining, or living room chair—soft or hard seat) at least 10 feet away and with enough space around it so that you can walk completely around it. Next select a soft chair or sofa (C4) that will be another 6-12 feet away.

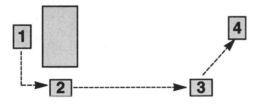

How to perform

Sit on chair C1 and start the timer. Stand and walk to C2, sit, and count to 3. Stand and walk to C3, sit, and count to 3. Stand, walk to and sit on C4, count to 3, stand, and return to C1. Stop the timer. Repeat 2 more times and use the mode or average score for your profile.

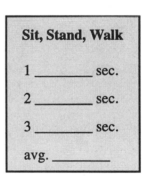

Variations

♦ Substitute sitting on the floor for one of the chair sits (to be done only by those who have leg strength to perform without risk of injury).

♦ Create your own sequence using the toilet, bed, floor, stairs, etc. Create a pattern you can use exactly the same each time. Practice every day and test yourself once a week.

Transferring objects

Transferring objects comprises grasping, lifting, lowering, and releasing of the objects. These actions usually are required activities of daily living for many women. We use combs, tooth brushes, cups, plates, food containers, clothes and numerous other articles which are grasped and transferred.

For this test, you will need 3 objects of different colors or labels but of the similar size and weight. You can use metal 12-15 oz. cans containing fruits, vegetables, or juice. You might also use socks or other cloth rolled or tied into a compact bundle suitable for grasping. You might use sports water bottles and fill to a chosen weight. Whatever you select, be sure you can grasp easily with one hand and also lift and lower it with ease.

How to perform

Place 2 objects on a counter and 1 on an overhead shelf. Label them #1 and #3 on the counter and #2 on the shelf. Stand facing counter, place the timer on the counter. Start the timer and grasp object #1 and place on shelf, grasp #2 on the shelf and lower it to the counter placing it next to #3. Grasp #3, lift it to the shelf and place it next to #1. Continue this sequence until each object has been lifted and lowered three times. Stop the timer and record the elapsed time.

Variations

◆ Increasing the weight of the objects

◆ Adding more shelf levels For example, you can transfer objects using a series of book shelves reaching to lower shelves and then to higher shelves

◆ Turning the object. For example, lift object to the shelf and then turned upside down. Turn object back over when lowing.

Practice every day or every second day and test yourself every week or two.

Balancing

Balance, which is both static and dynamic, refers to your ability to maintain control of your center of gravity with respect to your base of support. In other words, the balance point of your body will always be in a position relative to your feet so that you do not fall. With these series of tests, only static balance will be tested. Although you can move parts of the body to maintain balance, the feet cannot move, not even slide a bit.

One foot balance

Hold your timer in one hand and stand barefooted on a smooth surface. Evaluate your ability to balance through the following five ways: standing on preferred foot, the other foot, forefoot (balls) of both feet, forefoot of preferred foot, forefoot of the other. As you lift your foot from the floor, begin timing. Check the timer to see if 10 seconds has elapsed. If so, stop the timer and record a 10 in the chart below. If you lose your balance before 10 seconds have elapsed, stop the timer as soon as the raised foot touches the floor or your supporting foot moves. Repeat the test using the other foot.

Variations

- Change surface, e.g. soft carpet.
- Change footwear, e.g. sandals.
- Change surface and footwear.

Be sure to record the environment (footwear and surface) since your performance may not be the same in all environments. Practice balancing in different environments, everyday and test yourself every week.

Balancing Scores Record (10=Maximum Score)

Base of support	Duration	Foot used
preferred foot	_____	right ___ left ___
other foot	_____	right ___ left ___
forefoot of two feet	_____	
forefoot of preferred foot	_____	right ___ left ___
forefoot of other foot	_____	right ___ left ___

footwear _____   surface _____

Eye-hand-object coordination

We need to respond daily to moving objects. Whenever we cross a street, walk through a shopping mall parking area, or ride a bicycle, we make decisions based upon the speed of approaching cars and pedestrians. If an object begins to fall off a table, we react to catch it. And, of course, each time we participate in a ball-type sport, we respond to the moving ball.

Three choices are given: toss ball in air and catch, bounce ball against the floor and catch, throw against a wall and catch.

Toss and catch

Toss the ball and catch it with both hands as you sit or stand. After 20 catches, stop the timer and record your score. Vary the task by walking as you toss and catch for development of total body coordination.

Toss and Catch

1 _____ sec.

2 _____ sec.

3 _____ sec.

avg. _____

Bounce and catch

In a sitting or standing position, bounce and catch the ball. Choose a smooth, hard surface (possibly outside) for this test.

How to perform

Start the timer. Bounce and catch 20 times. Stop the timer and record your score. A variation on this is walking as fast as you can while bouncing the ball on one step and catching it on the next. Walk and bounce 10 times, turn, and return to the starting position, bouncing another 10 times. Stop the timer and record your score.

Throw against a wall

Stand facing a wall approximately 5 feet from it. Evaluate whether or not this distance is far enough away for you to throw the tennis ball at the wall and catch the rebounded ball repeatedly. If not, change the distance and remember it for future testing.

How to perform

The easiest task is to throw and catch whichever way you choose. A variation of this is to throw the ball with one hand and catch the ball with the other hand, then throw with that hand and catch with the first hand. Time how long it takes to throw and catch 20 times. Record your score. Repeat once or twice and figure the average time.

Manipulation

We move our hands and fingers during many tasks in which we manipulate objects in our environment. But how often do we analyze our movements to see if one or more of the fingers are ignored or disregarded? To maintain

*E*ye-hand-object *coordination activities will improve your perceptual motor skills.*

Bounce and Catch

1 _____ sec.

2 _____ sec.

3 _____ sec.

avg. _____

Throw and Catch

1 _____ sec.

2 _____ sec.

3 _____ sec.

avg. _____

functional use of both hands and all fingers, include the thumbs. This representative test requires a touch tone telephone, calculator, or typewriter, or you can use the numeric pad on a computer. Once again you will need a timer.

How to perform

Place the timer near the telephone. Start the timer and execute the following sequence as fast as possible:

♦ Using fingers 2, 3, and 4 of one hand press the 9 keys in sequential order alternating among the three fingers in each row. Repeat 4 times for a total of 5. Stop the timer at the completion of the 5 times.
   ♦ Repeat above using fingers 3, 4, 5.
   ♦ Repeat with fingers 1, 2, 3 (1 is thumb)

Manipulation Sequences Record			
time 1_____	time 2_____	time 3_____	fingers 3,4,5
time 1_____	time 2_____	time 3_____	fingers 3,4,5
time 1_____	time 2_____	time 3_____	fingers 1,2,3
time 1_____	time 2_____	time 3_____	fingers 1,2,3

Variations

There are unlimited ways to vary this finger dexterity action. Here are some suggestions:

♦ Reverse the sequences moving from right-to-left in each row (3-2-1)
   ♦ Press keys in reverse order (9-8-..)
   ♦ Change sequences to columns, sequencing as #s 1-4-7, 2-5-8, 3-6-9.
   ♦ Change the fingers used (fingers 1, 3, 5).

◆ Use a dial phone and dial sequence.

◆ Play a series of chords or scales on a musical instrument.

◆ Make shapes with clay or putty.

You may wish to select items on the self-appraisal test to practice everyday. In this way you can maintain your level of movement-fitness. Practice more and you can improve your performances and enhance your capacity for activities to enrich your life-space.

Many activities can be used for assessing and improving your movement capabilities, both in effectiveness and quality. You may also use and modify the many activities presented in other chapters of this book.

A self-appraisal test can also be used as an exercise program

Constructing your baseline profile

Construct a baseline profile to visualize your performance and compare to future profiles. A sample profile appears below with hypothetical scores. Use the profile charts on the following pages or create your own.

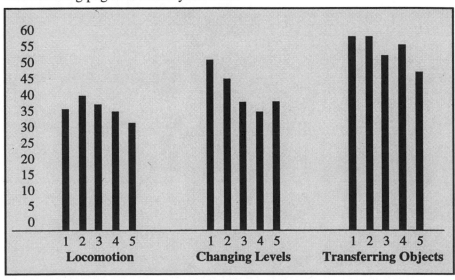

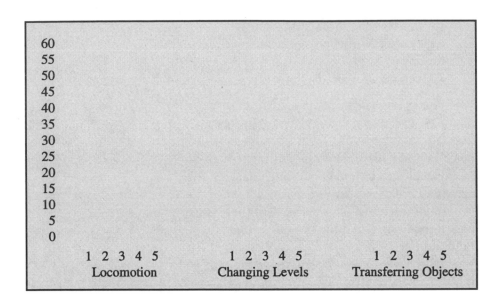

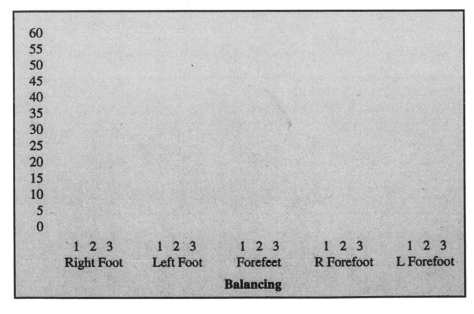

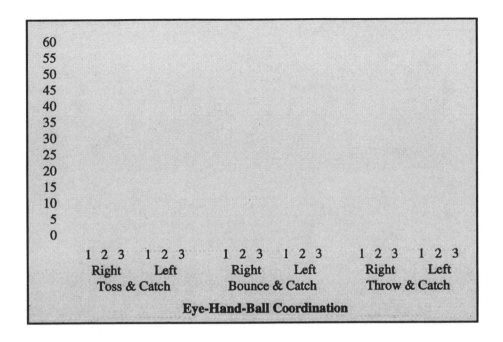

Chapter Five

Move All Your Bones

The foundation of movement is dependent upon the mobility of your joints. The amount of elasticity and stretch of your muscles, tendons, and ligaments will determine to a great extent just how flexible your joints are. Flexibility refers to the range of motion (ROM) capability. How far can you move the body parts that rotate about your joints? Anatomically, each joint permits movement in predetermined directions depending upon the bone configuration. The new-born child usually has the greatest range of motion of all age groups; thus, children are said to be very flexible. We lose some amount of flexibility and decrease our working range of motion as we begin to walk and develop many habitual patterns. Consequently, we choose to ignore many other patterns of movement.

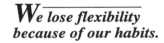

We lose flexibility because of our habits.

The middle-aged and older woman may become less flexible than younger women because of disuse, the aging changes associated with connective tissue, diseases (i.e., arthritis), and work postures. Since habitual stooped postures, for example, limit one's range of motion, women of all ages can experience loss of flexibility. Many fitness programs do not include joint fitness as a goal, but as a rule, flexibility exercises are used merely as warm-ups and are relegated to only a few body parts. We, however, cannot take for granted that we will move with ease and retain our childhood flexibility. Because the adult lifestyle tends to be one of sitting or standing and using the hands in front of the body, many young women will experience dysfunctional flexibility. In particular, there can be loss of arm movements behind the back and above the head resulting in dysfunctional flexibility at the shoulder. Persons in sitting jobs thus may show difficulty in reaching for objects in overhead cabinets or manipulating fasteners on the back of a blouse or brassiere.

Finger extension and foot mobility also have been observed to decrease due to the frequency of grasping activities and the wearing of stiff-soled or high-heeled shoes. Some styles of clothing also interfere with our ability to move well. The high technological society of today is in conflict with the maintenance of flexibility for our bodies.

Although such generalities concerning prevalent loss of flexibility can be applied to human beings as a whole, not all lose the same amount or the same types of mobility. For example, women who climb ladders to fight fires in five-story buildings do not lose their shoulder mobility. Badminton players develop fantastic flexibility in the hand, but only in one hand. Bread and pizza dough makers can rotate their forearms as well as they could when children. Women with a diversified lifestyle, trying new things at every opportunity, tend to maintain greater flexibility than persons with a routine of a few, selected activities, but no woman is completely immune to loss of flexibility.

Balanced flexibility

Posture

There is no question that inadequate flexibility results in postural problems, and conversely, postural habits create flexibility problems. If you stand with your body weight on one foot and hip, you will develop abnormal curvatures of the spine and one hip higher than the other. If you always sit with head flexed looking downward, you will develop the flexed head syndrome as you stand, walk, and sit doing other activities. If you spend much of your time sitting, you may begin to walk with a flexed trunk instead of standing tall.

Sports

If you play a sport, chances are you have greater than normal ROM/flexibility in some of your joints. Other joints, or muscles producing other movements at these joints, may not be activated. The javelin thrower who always throws with the same arm (for example, right arm) produces a lateral lean of the trunk (to the left) away from the throwing arm. This causes shortening of the muscles on her left side and lengthening of the muscles on her right side. Scoliosis, lateral curvature of the spine, could result if trunk flexion exercises to the right side are not practiced. Likewise, if you sit at an office job (computer keyboard operator) you are apt to have shortened anterior muscles across the chest and rounded shoulder and kyphotic back (humped appearance). The posterior muscles are lengthened. Thus, for every increased ROM in one direction, there is apt to be decreased ROM in the opposite direction. Specific exercises must be performed to obtain balanced flexibility.

Balanced flexibility gives you harmony of all your muscles with no excess shortening or lengthening.

Practice and perceive your joint fitness

Daily practice and periodic evaluation of your range of motion for every joint is a must. Only you can determine whether or not your joint fitness is adequate. When you do not perceive problems or limitations, you increase the risk of losing functional behavior and independence. Self-awareness of ROM capabilities can be developed through the use of a subjective self-perception rating scale known as the Perceived Resistance Rating. As you perform a movement you will rate it with respect to ease of movement and expansiveness of range. You also will compare movements of the right and left sides of your body. To start your program, perform all the possible movements of your body described in Chapter 1 and shown on the following charts.

U̲se a Perceived Resistance Rating to assess our ROM.

How to perform

◆ Perform the movement slowly and pause at the end of the movement, exhaling and then pushing farther (stretching) as you inhale and hold the new position and then exhale, inhale and stretch again on the inhalation, slowly return to the starting position.

◆ Repeat at least two more times

◆ Mentally rate the movement as to perceived difficulty, stiffness etc. Use a scale of 1-10, with 1 being easiest to move.

◆ Perform a few extra stretches with those movements perceived to be more than 5.

◆ Use the assessment charts which follow to guide you in remembering all the movement possibilities.

◆ If you feel any stiffness, tightness, lack of satisfactory range of motion, or other problems when performing any of the movements, place a check in the appropriate boxes in the charts.

Assessment Charts

Arm Movements
(perform standing with feet apart for balance)

	right	left
Sideward lift to above the head (abduction)	☐	☐
Forward lift to above the head (flexion)	☐	☐
Backward lift (extension) 45 degrees	☐	☐
Lift across body (adduction)	☐	☐
Inward rotation	☐	☐
Outward rotation	☐	☐

Forearm Movements
(perform standing or sitting)

	right	left
Flexion (touch hand to shoulder)	☐	☐
Extension (straighten arm)	☐	☐
Supination (palm upward)	☐	☐
Pronation (palm downward)	☐	☐

Shoulder Movements
(perform with arms relaxed at sides)

	right	left
Elevation (raise upward)	☐	☐
Forward and inward actions	☐	☐
Backward and inward actions	☐	☐
Circumduction (circling)	☐	☐

Hand Movements
(perform standing, lying, or sitting)

	right	left
Flexion (move palm toward forearm)	☐	☐
Extension (move back of hand toward forearm)	☐	☐
Circumduction (circling movement)	☐	☐
Abduction (sideward, thumb toward forearm)	☐	☐
Adduction (sideward, 5th finger toward forearm)	☐	☐
Finger spread and extension	☐	☐
Finger flexion	☐	☐

Head Movements
(perform sitting or standing)

	right	left
Rotation (look behind)	❑	❑
Tilt (bring ear toward shoulder)	❑	❑
Flexion (bring chin toward chest)	❑	
Extension (lifting upward and backward)	❑	

Trunk Movements
(perform standing with feet apart for balance)

	right	left
Side Flexion	❑	❑
Circumduction	❑	❑
Flexion (forward with head toward knees)	❑	
Extension (lying position is best)	❑	

Leg Movements
(perform sitting or lying)

	right	left
Sideward lift toward the head (adduction)	❑	❑
Forward lift to above the head (flexion)	❑	❑
Backward lift (extension) 30 degrees	❑	❑
Lift across body (adduction)	❑	❑
Inward rotation	❑	❑
Outward rotation	❑	❑
Circumduction	❑	❑
Lower leg flexion (touch foot to thigh)	❑	❑

Foot Movements
(perform sitting or lying)

	right	left
Flexion (point toes up)	❑	❑
Extension (straighten foot, pointing toes)	❑	❑
Circumduction (circling movement)	❑	❑
Eversion (turn foot sole outward)	❑	❑
Inversion (turn foot sole inward)	❑	❑
Toe spread and extension	❑	❑
Toe flexion	❑	❑

Guidelines

♦ Always move slowly; fast movement will elicit a stretch reflex and less movement r a n g e. You defeat your purpose of stretching.

♦ Use your arm or a partner to help you stretch further.

♦ Hold the stretch for a few seconds

♦ Tight joints need frequent stretching

Charting and planning your ROM program

Based upon your Perceived Resistance Rating (PRR) of all the possible movements of your body, organize a program for improvement of your range of motion (ROM). A partner can be very helpful, as can be organized yoga classes, a swimming pool or hot tub, and music. Some examples follow,

*P*erceive *the joy of stretching.*

Partner-assisted ROM exercises

Passive, or partner-assisted ROM exercises are those in which a partner moves the body part for you. This practice is very beneficial since you may relax and allow the stretch to take place. Your partner holds the body part and moves to the maximum range of motion, holding it for a few seconds and applying a slight pressure. Care must be taken that the partner does not hurt you. The movement should be made slowly, gradually taking the body part to its limit. You tell your partner when to stop. When you say "stop" because your pain tolerance has been reached, no further stretch should be made. There is no danger using this approach, since your psychological pain tolerance occurs prior to your physical pain tolerance; in other words, you perceive it to hurt before it actually hurts!

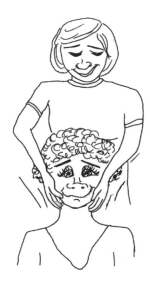

A partner can assist you in a *full body stretch,* that is, extending the spine. It is very difficult to do this effectively by yourself. Lie on the floor, a bed, or an air mattress. Your partner takes a position behind your head and places her hands on the sides of your head, with fingers along the jaw bone and palms covering your ears, as shown in the illustration. She gently pulls your head from your neck causing a stretch in the neck, chest, and lower back—the total spine. You will feel released from pressures and know the true feeling of a body stretch. You'll want this everyday!

Alternatively, this can be done while sitting on the floor. Your partner stands behind you and takes the same position on your head. The pull is now upward to produce the stretch. If a partner is not available, you can produce some stretch by yourself through imaging. Sit or stand and imagine the top of your head reaching for the ceiling or the sky. Think of your entire body being lifted upward, imagine you are at a chiropractor's office or being placed in traction. In fact, if you have ever had a neck problem which required you to receive traction, you know what it feels like to experience that wonderful release from the compression of gravity.

Improving ROM in a water media

Range of motion development for a chronic or injury condition is particularly easy to do in a water environment. Persons with muscle weaknesses or low strength find that movements in the water will have a positive effect upon their efforts to stretch. In particular, women suffering from arthritis will find the water medium to be the best place to exercise.

T̅ry stretching in swimming pools, hot tubs, or bathtubs.

The warm water has a relaxing effect and aids in reducing resistance to motion, thus facilitating exercise and stretching capabilities. Water has a second major benefit. Since water supports the body with its buoyancy force, the limbs require less muscle force to be moved.

Remember that all movements are to be done with the body part totally under water. Too often with water exercise programs the women are standing in the water, but their arms are moving in the air. Keep the body parts in the water!

Move slowly and follow the guidelines previously given. You can move to your heart's content without feeling afraid of hurting yourself.

If you know how to swim, you can do all your stretching while enjoying swimming. You must, however, perform several swimming strokes. The front crawl includes stretches that are different from the back crawl. The scissors kick, breast stroke kick and flutter kicks also provide new stretches. As you swim, be expansive: stretch on the glides, reach on the pulls, emphasize foot action, do different styles of sculling, and don't be afraid to create your own stroke variations. Avoid thinking of swimming as fast as possible or applying a great deal of force in the strokes. Rather, swim with the joy of stretching.

Think of being a fish in the water. Undulate your body as fishes do when they swim. The water is a perfect media for producing a flow of energy moving from head to foot and generating flexibility in the spine. Swimmers have used this undulation when swimming the butterfly dolphin and using the dolphin kick. But you can promote total body undulation with a dolphin action.

Swimming can be one of the best activities for improving and maintaining flexibility.

Improving ROM on land

In your home or that of a friend, enjoy moving in all directions and discover the capabilities of your body in space by using music, a mirror, meditation, or imagery. Here are some suggestions:

 ◆ Look at yourself in a mirror and pretend your mirror image is your twin. You both can move together. Try to do something your twin cannot do—smile.
 ◆ With a friend, perform ROM movements as shadows of each other. You move and she is your shadow. Then she moves and you shadow.
 ◆ Move with a background of relaxing, soothing, meditative or ecologically themed music. Classical music also is usually excellent for practicing ROM movements.

*F*lexibility is influenced by body proportions and circumferences.

Body size and shape and flexibility

Once again your body characteristics must be considered, since your body size, proportionality, body weight and body musculature affect your flexibility. Your flexibility will be different compared to another person's, but it may be suitable for the uniqueness of you. The truth of this concept is evident when we look at the normative tests of flexibility. These often are biased since they are designed to test your movement relative to another body part. For example, how many times has someone said to you, "Touch the floor with your hands by bending over from the standing position. Do not bend your knees?" This is not a valid test of your flexibility, since you may have extra short arms and extra long legs. Such a test becomes a test of body proportionality.

The following two flexibility tests are useful for evaluating trunk flexibility and arm-shoulder flexibility. They can be performed periodically—every two weeks or every month—or as daily practice activities to maintain/improve flexibility.

Sit and reach forward

Sit with your legs extended and trunk erect (vertical). Place a yardstick (ruler) between your legs from the knees to beyond the feet. Place your fingers lightly on the ruler and begin to flex the trunk, reaching forward with the fingers until you reach as far as you can. Hold and read the value at which your fingers rest on the ruler (e.g. 26 inches). Record this as your flexibility score. Repeat.

Forward Reach

Trial 1_____

Trial 2_____

Trial 3_____

Over the shoulder greet your fingers

Reach up behind the back with the left hand. With the right arm, reach over the shoulder with elbow upward and fingers behind your back. Try to touch fingers. If they touch, place a check under R on the chart on the following page.

If you could not touch your fingers, ask someone to measure the distance between fingers with a ruler. Record (under R) to the half inch the distance between fingertips.

Now reach behind with the right arm and over the shoulder with the left. Place a check under L if you touched fingertips, or record the distance between fingertips. Compare the two positions. Is one more difficult than the other? Now try to reach farther. Can you touch past the first digit, past the second digit, touch the palm, or grasp hands? This test is one of the most effective ways to reveal asymmetry in our bodies.

Behind the Back Reach								
(Right=right above, left below Left=left above, right below)								
	R	L		R	L		R	L
fingertips	___	___	first digit	___	___	second digit	___	___
palm	___	___	mid palm	___	___	grasp hands	___	___

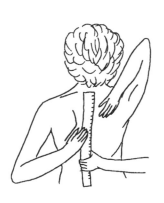

*C*heck your
bilateral symmetry.

Do not be upset if you cannot touch your fingertips. The width of your shoulders is one determining factor in your success; if your shoulders are wide, you will have to move your hands to the left and right to be able to touch. This makes it harder than for a narrower-shouldered woman. Muscle and fat volume are also factors which determine whether or not your fingers touch. Arthritis, old injuries, and shortened pectoral muscles (anterior chest muscles from habitual flexed sitting position) inhibit performance. Assessing and recording progress in improvement of flexibility and comparisons between right and left abilities are very important.

Final Guidelines

♦ Become aware of your ROM by frequently using the Perceived Resistance Rating as you perform all possible movements.

♦ Practice movements which you perceive as being difficult to perform—high PRR.

♦ Emphasize practice with feet, hands, trunk.

♦ Emphasize all directions and both right and left body parts.

♦ Emphasize maintaining extension movements.

♦ At first the sign of loss of ROM, increase the DIF of those movements. Reminder—DIF means duration, intensity and frequency.

Chapter Six

Use Your Muscles

Because we live on Earth our muscles must be strong enough to lift the weight of our body or the body parts we move. This occurs with every movement and is referred to as overcoming our inertia "the tendency not to move" or to keep moving once we begin to move. The more our our individual parts and our total body weighs, the stronger our muscles must be to effectively produce movement. Therefore, the more you weigh, the more work you perform. For example, if you weigh 150 pounds and walk 20 feet, you would perform 3,000 ft lbs of work. If, however, you weigh 100 lbs, you would perform only 2,000 ft lbs of work. Therefore, the heavier person requires greater musculature to do the same activity as a lighter weight person.

Minimal strength fitness is general strength to move your body. You determine what is minimum strength for you. This depends upon what you want or need to be able to do: walk through the grocery store, climb stairs to your office, rise from a chair, run across the street, play tennis and etc.

Muscle requirements are determined in part by body weigh.

Conversely, the more muscular strength you have, the more active you can make your lifestyle. You want your minimum muscular strength to include a reservoir for emergencies and unexpected, enjoyable leisure activities and opportunities. Thus, it is important to develop your muscles, since you'll have less excess baggage to carry around. If you have 20% muscle compared to 10% muscle, you will have an easier job moving your body. You will feel more energized and better able to cope with some of the stresses of life.

Naturally, we use our bodies to move and manipulate objects. Do we carry groceries, shovel snow, rake the lawn, push a lawn mower, knead bread, operate a non-electric typewriter, chop wood, operate a

*Muscle
requirements
are related to
what you want
or need to do.*

loom, push a vacuum cleaner, etc. with ease? We need to develop muscular fitness specific to the activities of our lifestyle. We need to acquire muscular strength, including endurance and power, in all the 72 major muscles which pull on our bones to produce movements. One or two strength exercises will not do this.

How much muscular strength do you need? It depends. Norms, based upon age or gender, and even fitness level, are misleading and not reflective of your lifestyle. If you believe that, as a woman, you are only two-thirds as strong as a man, you may be wrong, especially if you work as a telephone line repairperson. Although, the average woman (whomever she is) is two-thirds as strong as the average man (again, who is this?), not all men are stronger than all women, especially when each muscle group is evaluated. In 1977 a woman weight lifter (114 lb. category) broke the men's record (in the same body-weight category) by lifting 225 lbs. That's almost twice her body weight! We know that the leg strength of trained men and women may be similar between the genders. How we use our body, as well as how much testosterone and other genetic material we have are major factors in determining which women and which of their muscles develop great strength and which do not. Women have testosterone too!

How to develop muscular fitness

Lifting, pushing and pulling activities are common daily living tasks requiring muscle force—in each situation, there is a resistance which must be overcome. The resistance is your body weight, someone else's body weight or an external weight or load (i.e., bag of groceries, hand weights). You use some of your muscles everyday and in this way maintain their level of muscular fitness. Other muscles are left in disuse and, when needed, will not be effective in unfamiliar actions. How do you develop a greater level of muscular fitness? Activities must be performed that overload the system. This means that:

◆ To change the muscle, repeat an activity until you feel a slight tiredness and then repeat at least once more.

◆ To gain muscular strength, perform activities requiring high muscle force and repeat 3-5 times.

◆ To gain muscular endurance, perform activities using moderate muscle force and repeat 20-40 times.

◆ To gain muscular power, perform activities using little-to-moderate force and repeat as fast as safely possible.

Selecting different activities can reduce boredom, help to achieve more natural movement, and develop varying degrees of power, strength, and endurance specific to your needs.

There are many places and ways to practice activities for developing muscular fitness. For example, you can practice at home, riding in your car, sitting or standing on a subway train, at work and at a fitness club. You can practice via the following ways:

◆ Using your own body for the resistance.

◆ Using a partner to regulate resistance.

◆ Using commercially available or self-fabricated devices.

◆ Using ergometers or other large exercise machines.

Everyone's muscles respond uniquely to exercise—for maximum benefit individualize resistance, duration, repetition, & speed of movement.

Use of your body

Your body is always with you and is therefore a natural for you to use in developing your muscles anytime, anyplace. Using your body is the most common, but not always the most effective, way to develop muscular fitness. Static and dynamic muscle force can be produced while moving in all directions and using all body parts as described in the preceding chapter. To maintain and develop the muscular strength you can perform the activities of range of motion slowly lifting each body part in a specified direction, but always against gravity, and doing 10 or more repetitions, if possible. If your muscles are "fit" you should be able to do this without any aches or tiredness. If some muscles react with soreness or "why did you wake me up?" think of them as "lost muscles" that need to be developed. Record those actions that you perceived to be performed by "lost muscles." The lost muscles can benefit through further practice. Lift the body part many times, in the morning, during the day and at night. Just learn to use/move your body!

A push-up is not a push-up is not a push-up is not a push-up.

Some strength improvement can be obtained merely from moving your body—walking, climbing stairs, doing sit-ups, and high stepping. Whenever you lift a body part upward you oppose the force of gravity and need to contract your muscles. Muscles will maintain their original strength or improve in strength if you increase the number of times you perform your activity.

There is a major disadvantage in using only the body as the resistance, since there can be no progression in amount of resistance. Furthermore, the body usually weighs so much that a person cannot perform more than one lift, push or pull. Often, even one action may not be possible because you begin with too high a resistance. For example, if you are asked to perform a push-up with feet and hands on the floor, do you know that you need to lift 70% of your total body weight? Thus if you weigh 135 lbs, you would need at least 94 lbs of arm muscle force. Can you lift 90 lbs? More than 3 times? Airplane luggage has a maximum weight limit of 88 lbs. What does that tell you concerning the intensity of push-ups?

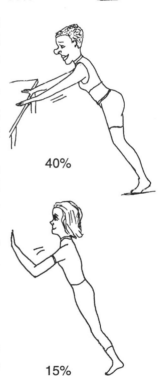

50%

40%

15%

To confound the situation further, you are in a compromised position with arms flexed maximally when starting to push-up. This starting position places the muscles in mechanically disadvantaged angles of pull. When muscle force is exerted to push the body upward, much of the force will be lost in directions other than upward. Thus, much more than 94 lbs of force is required. What does that tell you concerning push-ups? Push-ups are difficult!

For a realistic approach to development of arm and shoulder girdle strength, variations of this full length (original) push-up can be used. Note from the illustrations how the resistance to be lifted changes appreciably as you modify the push-up. If you want to use push-ups as a means of strength improvement, select the type of push-up equal to your current abilities.

Alternatives or modifications of the original push-up are realistic.

The same problem of an unrealistic overloading with the push-up is also present when attempting to do chin-ups and sit-ups. Even arm lifts and leg lifts may be overloading weak musculature if you have heavy arms and legs. There are many variations of all these exercises. You can place your arms along the side of the body and lift only the head and shoulders for a shoulder sit-up rather than a full trunk sit-up. You can practice sit-downs and not go all the way to the floor. Set your own goals and create your own variations! Remember too, that your achievements cannot be directly compared to achievements of others. If you do 4 sit ups and your friend does 10, your performances may be equivalent. How much work did you do and how much muscle mass do you have? Body weight and amount of musculature must be factored into the equation of intensity of strength training and expected performance.

Static strength development

Some strength training can be done against your own resistance. For example, hold the left forearm with your right hand and resist the flexion of the left forearm as you try to raise the left hand to the shoulder. The muscle will contract, but no movement will occur if you resist with your right hand more than the left forearm muscles can overcome. You can easily do this if you lean your upper body weight on the forearm. The left forearm muscles will develop strength only at the position being held. This is termed isometric strength development.

Static contractions of each group of muscles can be done when lying in bed, as well as sitting or standing. Muscle force is gained only at the contracting position, not throughout the

Inhale and exhale as you perform isometrics.

total range of motion unless a series of static contractions are made. When performing the static contractions (termed isometrics), hold the contraction a short time 1-3 breathing cycles (inhalations and exhalations). Remember to consciously breathe. You can create a series of isometric contractions and develop muscle strength throughout the ROM if you:

♦ Assume a new position, angle at the joint, and repeat the isometric contraction.

♦ Assume another position, and repeat.

♦ Repeat until the entire range of motion has been utilized.

Partner resistance

This is one of the best ways to develop an awareness of muscle strength and to know your body and its capabilities. You also help others to appreciate their strength or needs. When you work together, you both benefit. You also can have a great social/personal experience. One caution is to take care to regulate the resistance, progressing from virtually no resistance to the movement of the exercising body part to maximum resistance, at which time no movement of the exercising body part occurs. Gradual increments of resistance should occur, especially at the starting position when resistance cannot be easily tolerated. Strength can be achieved without danger if these procedures are followed, and strength development can be fun.

Full range of movement of the body part can be regulated so that the muscle contracts throughout the movement. At any position, resistance can be increased or decreased. This results in strength gains at every body position of the limb.

Guidelines for partner-applied resistance

♦ Apply no force and allow partner to move through full ROM.
♦ Apply slight force for relatively easy movement through ROM.
♦ Increase force and slow the movement and continue to allow movement at a constant velocity (isokinetic concept).
♦ Increase the force until movement is very difficult and, when no movement occurs, reduce force and allow a short distance of movement, increase force again to create a static contraction, continue until full ROM is completed.

Partner-applied resistance can result in gains in muscular strength, but gains in muscular power or endurance are not so easily practiced with a partner. A partner may tire before the exerciser does, or one of you could be injured.

Use of resistance devices

In order to vary the resistance and overload the muscle effectively in a short period of time, resistive devices can be bought or fabricated, and creatively used.

Hand held devices

♦ Household objects—cans of food, plastic bottles of liquid, hammers, pots with objects inside, sockful of flatware or sand, metal piping.
♦ Commercially available objects—hand weights, aquatic resistance devices.

Limb attached devices

◆ Weighted straps and pouches, commercially available, or fabricated from cloth or canvas with dried peas, sand, gravel, lead fishing weights, bolts and screws, or cans of food inside strapped to body parts.

◆ Two weighted socks tied together and draped over wrist or ankle or other body parts.

◆ Weighted gloves or mittens.

Body trunk devices

◆ Weight belts, back pack, pack vest.

◆ Heavy winter clothing worn on body.

Resistive cables and tubing

◆ Stretch cords or rubber tubing held in hands, under feet, or attached to doors.

◆ Pulley cables with pulleys attached at top of door, cable with weight on one side and cable for person to pull on other side.

Sequence of strength training by varying the distance of resistance

Increased weight is not necessary to gain strength; the same weight moved farther from the joint will also produce a gain in strength.

The biceps brachii and brachial radials cross the elbow and are strengthened in the resistive movement of forearm flexion. They will work the hardest if the device is worn at the wrist than in any other position on the forearm. This is known as the law of moment arms and leverage. The muscle force required to hold, move or lift the resistance device is directly related to the distance the device is placed from the involved joint. Thus, when the forearm moves at the elbow joint, less muscle force is required with the device strapped two inches from the elbow than if the device is strapped at the wrist.

When, however, the device is held in the hand, the muscles crossing the wrist become involved and the hand may fatigue before the muscles of the forearm are overloaded. Know which muscles are to be developed and select the position of the devices and the posture and movement of the body so that the appropriate muscles will be required to produce force. This can easily be done by palpating the muscle (touching and perceiving hardness of muscle).

Sequence of strength development by varying the amount of resistance

The amount of muscle force required to lift an object is directly proportional to the weight of this object. Thus, another way to develop strength is to increase the weight as your muscles become stronger and stronger.

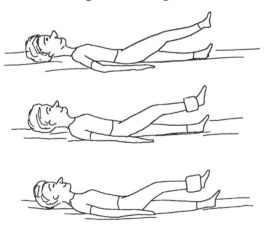

Ergometers, free weights, and weight machines

There are other ways to develop strength than by varying the distance the weight is from the joint and increasing the weight itself. A common way is to increase the number of repetitions, the speed, or the weight, or change two or more of these factors in various combinations. Products such as ergometers can be purchased in order to measure work and power. Some devices have microprocessors, computers, or a digital display and memory of your work and power, as well as such factors as duration of exercise, estimated calories burned and heart rate. Don't be fooled by all this high technology. Some of the data are not the truth. Assumptions are made that you represent an average, well-skilled, optimally efficient performer. We all know that an elite swimmer can use much less muscle effort and burn fewer calories than a novice swimmer who may perform many extraneous, but forceful, movements.

These performance-measuring devices, however are useful, since you can compare your progress or maintenance of your status. The actual numbers are not as important as the comparison of subsequent numbers on future performances. Use yourself as the criterion and profile yourself on strength as you did on the self-appraisal activities in Chapter 4.

Weight machines include individual single-function machines, dual-function, and multi-function machines, as well as a station consisting of many single-function machines. The single-function machines are preferred by many because they are easier to use and it takes less time to perform strength exercises for the major muscle groups. The multi-function machines require a rather complex changing of the machine, including the addition of attachments, in order to use the same machine for many muscle groups. If you are buying your own machines, you probably will "put up" with the time required to set up your machine for each muscle group in order to be financially able to purchase home equipment.

Free weights are those weights not held in your hands, but attached to a bar. You lift the bar with the appropriate amount of weight. The bar itself may be sufficient weight for initial free weight practice. Until you recognize your limits and know that you are safe using free weights, you should have a spotter working with you. Whenever you attempt a heavier weight or "one last lift," it is advisable to have a spotter to assist as you approach your maximum effort. The advantage of free weights as compared to weight machines is that more muscles are involved in each lift and body balance and coordination are developed along with muscular strength. The advantage of weight machines is that safety is regulated more through the machine's configuration than through the responsibility of the lifter.

Strengthen the total body and all its muscles

Whatever strength training method you use, all muscles need to be considered. At the end of this chapter are descriptions of movements to be used for activating the following muscle groups.

Legs—extensors, flexors, adductors, abductors. The latter two are essential; they rarely get used and are important as stabilizers, for posture, and for sports. Women with extra body weight need to work all 4 muscle groups for strong legs.

Arms—extensors, flexors, forearm rotations. The latter are used in turning door knobs, executing the smash in badminton and wringing water from clothes. Women usually do not develop the extensors; therefore, extension exercises need to be emphasized.

Trunk—flexors and extensors. The latter usually are weak and need extra development. Abdominals and obliques are essential to protect the lower back and keep proper pelvic tilt.

Shoulder girdle—Anterior, posterior, and scapular muscles.

Hands—flexor muscles are required for stronger finger and hand grip, Extensors need to be developed to counterbalance all flexion movements in our lives.

Feet—intrinsic muscles of foot, flexors, extensors, invertors, and evertors all need to be strengthened. A special section follows because the feet are so important and are so neglected.

R̲emember, your feet are your foundation.

A program for your feet

Be kind to your feet; they are the bases of support for your body and for you to move from place to place. When your feet hurt, find out the cause immediately—don't wait for blisters, bunions, or tendonitis to develop. Protect your feet so you do not have to treat them with medicine. Your feet are the foundation for all your locomotion, so keep them healthy.

◆ If you have sore feet, aching legs or low back pain from wearing ill-fitting shoes, whether high-heeled or not, change your shoes.

O̲u̲r̲ ̲e̲n̲j̲o̲y̲m̲e̲n̲t̲
in any physical
activity can
be partially
determined
by the condition
of our feet.

♦ Select shoes in which your toes lie flat and you can move all your toes.

♦ Select shoes that do not cause pressure or trauma to any part of your feet.

♦ Select shoes that are flexible enough so that forefoot action (flexing and extending) takes place easily during walking. Don't use stiff soled shoes.

♦ Walk barefoot or in comfortable low-heeled shoes or sandals a couple hours each day.

♦ Do foot exercises at home.

Activities with the feet: exercise barefoot! You need to be able to move all toes and exercise the arches of the feet. This may be done while lying, sitting or standing. The two major goals of these exercises are to increase flexibility and to develop the musculature of the feet.

For flexibility

♦ Move your feet as mentioned in Chapter One; moving them in all possible directions. Move slowly and hold terminal positions to cause a stretch.

♦ Ask a friend to gently move your feet slowly in each direction and hold for 3-5 seconds at the limits of movement. For example, push your foot downward and hold.

♦ Pick up a sock with your toes and transfer the sock from one foot to the other. Practice this a couple of times.

♦ While sitting, put soles of the feet together with lateral edges of feet on floor; next place medial edges on floor. Alternate several times.

♦ Walk on your heels lifting your toes as high as possible, thus, stretching the Achilles tendon; next walk on balls of feet lifting heels as high as possible. Alternate 10 steps each.

For strength

◆ In sitting position, place the sole of one foot on top of the instep of the other. Attempt to dorsi-flex (push toward your knee) the bottom foot while applying resistance with the other (plantar-flexing).

◆ An alternative exercise for plantar flexion strength is to use a towel as a stirrup around the ball of the foot. In a sitting position, hold the towel at each end and exert pressure against the mid-section of towel with the foot, attempting to plantar flex (extend) the foot.

◆ Ask a friend to apply pressure against the instep of the foot, and you attempt to dorsi-flex the foot (bring toes toward knee).

◆ Stand on both feet and rise onto the balls of the feet.

◆ Repeat previous activity wearing a back-pack of books or with some other weighted object.

Using fitness machines

If you go to a health club, there will be experts to help you use strength machines and describe the muscle groups to be developed. Reading health and fitness magazines also will be valuable in your quest for muscle fitness. This keeps you from being bored with the same exercises over and over.

One major advantage of weight machines is that you can measure what you do. You lift 40 pounds four times, half a foot (.05) each time, rest and repeat. This means you were able to lift 40 ft. x .05 lb. x 4 x 2 or a total of 160 ft. lbs.

If developing power, your progress can be measured by dividing the work done by the amount of time to complete the work:

Working with machines is fun because you can measure your progress.

160 ft. lbs. / 8 seconds
= 20 ft. lb.// sec.
or 0.04 horsepower or 30 watts

You will not be as powerful as an automobile engine, or even a lawnmower, motor boat or rototiller engine. We are equivalent to motors which drive model railroad trains or the turntable of a phonograph record player.

What do you, as a woman, need?

Since most of our forceful movements occur as flexion movements of the arms, legs and trunk, we need to emphasize the following strength development: extension of fingers, extension of arms, upper back extension, adduction of legs, extension of thighs, abdominal muscles and foot muscles.

I would estimate that ninety percent of women need to increase strength of their triceps muscles (arm extension), abdominal muscles, and posterior back muscles. The triceps is the balance to the biceps. The other two muscle groups are important for establishing posture and prevention of low back pain.

Above all, balance in muscle strength is a necessity for a harmonious body. What you do for the right side of the body, you should do for the left side of the body. What you do for the flexor group of muscles, you should do for the extensor group of muscles.

Muscular balance is key to a woman's symmetry & harmony.

Strength is for you:

♦ To defend yourself.
♦ To do your activities of daily living, including work.
♦ To have energy for fun.
♦ To feel good about yourself.

Movement descriptions

Muscles contract and are strengthened relative to the movements that you perform. The adductor muscles are strengthened when adduction movements are made; flexors are strengthened through flexion movements, extensors through extension movements, etc. You will always have more muscles contracting than you think, since additional muscles will also contract to stabilize other body parts and prevent extraneous movements.

Basic movements of Chapter One, as shown below, can be performed with elastic cords which offer resistance to the movement. Select the resistance you prefer and repeat each movement according to your comfort level and personal goals.

Strengthen arm extensors and upper body flexors and adductors.

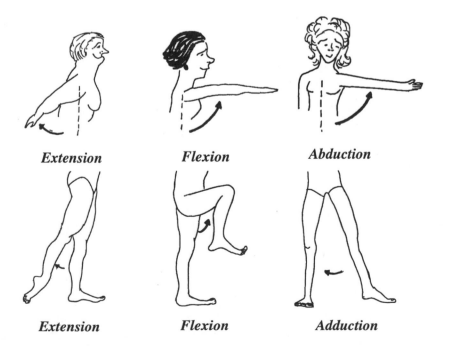

Extension	Flexion	Abduction

Extension	Flexion	Adduction

Chapter Seven

Expand Your Rivers of Life

The cardiovascular-respiratory systems are called the rivers of life. Blood and air flow from one place to another throughout our bodies, enabling us to function. Blood carries the food nutrients to cells, such as muscle cells, to produce energy for movement. Air is taken into the lungs and oxygen is absorbed into the blood and carried to all cells so that the energy producing cycle can operate. It makes sense that we need to develop strong, healthy, capable lungs, heart and blood vessels. We can do this via aerobic and anaerobic types of activities, commonly termed aerobic and anaerobic exercise.

Aerobic exercise is also known as endurance or stamina producing activity. Development of aerobic functioning results in increased ability to be active for long periods of time. You could paddle a canoe, walk, jog, or lift sacks of potatoes for an hour or more and not feel exhausted. In practical terms, you would be able to complete a day of physical work without becoming fatigued.

Anaerobic exercise is known as explosive activity. Development of anaerobic functioning results in an increase in your power and ability to perform high intensity efforts for short periods of time. For example, you would be able to run very fast across a busy street and repeat that quick effort several times. Anaerobic exercise produces no significant increase in endurance.

Will the activity effect a change?

Both aerobic and anaerobic activities are important.

With both types of activities, your heart rate and breathing rate will increase above that which normally occurs during sleeping, sitting, standing and daily non-physical type work. An expansion of your rivers of life can then take place. If there is no such increase, maintenance is all that will happen. Many women have a lifestyle in which maintenance is not rewarding enough. There is a feeling that you want to do more, enjoy life more, and move your body with joy. But, of course, there is some anxiety or fear of the unknown as your heart rate and breathing increase to unfamiliar levels. You may begin to sweat and feel uncomfortable. You may think the effort is too great. That is why you learn to accept and love your body enough to want it to become an integrated part of you, not merely an encasement by which you can move in this world. Your body is YOU!

Aerobics are enduring; anaerobics are high-intensity.

Have you ever thought what it would be like not to have a body? Think of the wildest science fiction stories of people in the outer galaxy with highly developed intellect, but only existing as energy—a light source or wisp of smoke—without shape or material body. But you have a body and it needs to be continually challenged and used or it can atrophy and become a hindrance rather than being an empowerer.

We need to consider self-awareness once again if we are to expand our rivers of life. There are many ways to do this, depending upon how objective, quantitative, or structured you wish to be. I would propose four ways to assess your physiological level of cardiovascular-respiratory functioning:

◆ Perceived exertion.
◆ Measuring heart rate across activities.
◆ Use target heart rate to estimate exertion.
◆ Compare perceived exertion and target heart rate.

Perceived exertion

Keep a log of how you perceive daily activities to affect fast breathing and blood flow. Use words relevant to you, or a more standard scale— 1) no effort 2) bit of effort 3) moderate 4) hard 5) very difficult

I would suggest using a 5 point scale no matter which words you use to describe your intensity level. In the chart below, identify your perception of the following activities:

Activity		Rating				Comments
standing	1	2	3	4	5	
walking	1	2	3	4	5	
stair climbing	1	2	3	4	5	
washing clothes	1	2	3	4	5	
vacuuming	1	2	3	4	5	
painting walls	1	2	3	4	5	
sitting - reading	1	2	3	4	5	
taking a shower	1	2	3	4	5	
playing softball	1	2	3	4	5	
playing the piano	1	2	3	4	5	
running	1	2	3	4	5	
bicycling	1	2	3	4	5	
toting children	1	2	3	4	5	
grocery shopping	1	2	3	4	5	
work activities	1	2	3	4	5	
other (list)	1	2	3	4	5	

*S*ense the
beating of
your heart.

If your ratings of your activities are always below 3, your rivers of life are at high risk of drying up. Soon you may not be able to maintain your lifestyle with pleasure, but are generating pre-mature aging. If your ratings are always in the middle, you probably will maintain your level of functioning. Those activities rated 4 or 5 are possible activities for aerobic enhancement of your rivers of life. Try to fit them into your lifestyle more frequently.

Measuring heart rate

In order to be more precise and quantify what is happening as you engage in activities of daily living, work and leisure, you will want to measure your heart rate. The heart rate is easy to calculate and your assessment of effort is a numerical value. Breathing rate is more difficult to measure, and not as directly related to the effort or level of exertion as is heart rate.

How to measure your heart rate

Use your index and middle fingers of one hand to press lightly on the radial artery on the inside of your other forearm just above the wrist and lateral to the tendons running the length of the forearm. An alternate way is to apply the light pressure on your carotid artery in the neck just below your chin. If you have difficulty in finding your pulse, you can use a heart rate monitoring device. Various types are available and some are built into exercise machines. Models for home use are also available. Heart monitoring devices are diverse in cost and type and may attach to the ear lobe, to the chest, or be grasped with your hands. The advantage of using these devices is that you can monitor while you are being active. When you are using your fingers to feel the pulsing of the blood, you may have to do so after the activity ceases. In this case, monitor your heart rate immediately. Determine the number of beats per minute (bpm). Do this by observing the second hand on a clock or watch, or have a friend work with you to time while you count. If you count 60 in 60 seconds it will be recorded as 60 bpm. You need not count for the entire minute. In fact, if the activity results in heart rates 20 bpm above your sitting heart rate, you will want to time for only 6 seconds. Then the number of beats you counts will be multiplied by 10 to obtain bpm. However you chose to do the monitoring, be consistent. Use the same time period whenever monitoring your heart rate.

Monitor heart rate while still in bed, after standing for five minutes, and after easy walking.

Construct a chart similar to the perceived exertion chart and record your heart rates. You also can use the same chart and write the heart rate in the comments column. Check and see the range of heart rates in your lifestyle activities. If the spread is no more than 20bpm you do not have enough change-producing activities for your rivers of life. You can safely incorporate such activities by performing your normal activities slightly faster and/or for a longer period of time. Remember, DIF? The duration, frequency and intensity should be elevated to produce change. If producing change is scary, only do so gradually and with the thought that it is for the enrichment of your life. You are working toward acquiring extra energy to enjoy being with friends and family, to engage in fun activities and to cope with unexpected physical efforts.

Using a target heart rate

It is common practice to calculate a target heart rate and use that as the criterion for measuring whether or not an activity will result in aerobic enhancement. Here is one method of determining your target heart rate:

◆ 220 minus age = predicted max. heart rate
◆ Predicted max. heart rate x .55 = minimum of target heart rate zone
◆ Predicted max. heart rate x .9 = maximum of target heart rate zone
◆ Select mid-zone for initial aerobic workout if healthy; otherwise, use a lower value

Example—Age 30

220-30 = 190 bpm predicted maximum
190 x .55 = 104
190 x .9 = 171
target heart rate = 135—140 bpm

This target heart rate will be greater than that of your basal heart rate, which is your resting heart rate as you lie in bed (50 bpm for very fit, 80 bpm for less fit). Your target heart rate will be higher than heart rate during most normal activities of daily living, such as sitting or standing (10-20% above the resting) or while walking normally (possibly 110-120 bpm).

Your goal, based upon the target heart rate, is to engage in activities during which your heart rate will be in the calculated zone once a day for 15 minutes or a total of 30 minutes during the day. Do you feel comfortable raising your heart rate to this level? If you are basically a sedentary person, you may feel that this target heart rate is too high a goal. For example, if all your daily activities are performed at heart rates

*R*emember, *target heart rate calculations are based upon the average person— since you are unique, use them as a guide only.*

under 120bpm and your target heart rate was calculated to be 140bpm, you might find this difference to be great. You might rather strive for 130bpm. There is no magic number, There is a continuum of moving from one exertion level to a higher one.

Remember that the target heart rate calculations are based upon assumptions of what the average person your age can and should do. Since you are unique, use the target heart rate as a guide.

Perceived exertion and target heart rate comparisons

If you prefer to link the subjectivity of perceived exertion to the objectivity of the target heart rate, you can elect to assess yourself using the approach shown below:

◆ Place a numerical value on the activity relative to your perceived exertion. Various scales have been devised based upon the work of Borg and include values from 1-20, 10-20, or similar.

Match your heart rate to perception of exertion.

◆ Start your activity and continue for beyond two minutes, the short-term adaptation period in which your body systems adapt.

◆ After 3-5 minutes or longer, take note of how your body feels (perceived exertion level) based upon the heart beat and breathing rate.

◆ Stop and immediately measure your heart rate.

◆ Write the values in the following chart.

◆ Repeat this procedure for a variety of activities, such as the ones you wrote in the first chart in this chapter.

Comparing Perceived Exertion & Measured Heart Rate		
Perception of effort	*Scale*	*Measured heart rate*
easy	1-9	
moderate	10-11	
moderate-hard	12-13	
somewhat hard	14-15	
hard	16-17	
very hard	18-19	
exhausting (maximum)	20	

This scale is useful since heart rates vary with activities. You can become your own evaluator and not need to rely on a timer. You also become more aware of how your body responds to physical activity. Take your body to a more intense level than your daily activities normally take you!

What aerobic activities are best for you?

Regardless of what others tell you, the best aerobic activity is the one you will enjoy. You must like the activity, or your perception of its rewards, in order to practice it as part of your lifestyle. There are two basic categories of aerobic activities: repetitive and non-repetitive.

Repetitive aerobic activities

◆ Walking—fast enough to breathe deeply, but can still talk.

◆ Jogging—slow enough to continue for 15 min.

◆ Walk/jog—combine to elevate heart rate.

◆ Running—a pace you can keep for 15 min.

◆ Grocery walking—walk all the aisles of a grocery store and then select products.

◆ Bicycle—ride using a gear that makes you work.

◆ Stationary bike—ride with resistance.

◆ Stepper—use a stepping machine.

◆ Rowing machine—or row, or canoe.

◆ Climber—use a climbing machine that is an arm and leg exerciser.

◆ Skier—use a cross country ski machine or slalom skier.

◆ Swimming—lap swimming.

The above examples of repetitive, cyclic activities may become boring. Therefore, you may wish to use two or more of them. You may prefer to engage in these activities while watching television, listening to the radio, meditating or doing something with part of your mind while reducing stress in the rest of you. The use of these repetitive activities is popular, however, for those of us who want to measure what we do. You know how much effort you made, since the number of minutes, the distances, or other measurable parameters can be used to quantify your workout. For example, using a fitness stepper machine, you stepped 1,236 steps during the 15 minute period with a post-exercise heart rate of 140 beats per minute (bpm). The total work done was 1,236 x distance of step-up (.5 feet) which is equal to 618 foot pounds of work. The next day, you repeated the same number of steps and had a post-exercise heart rate of 138 bpm. Your aerobic ability has improved, since you can perform the same exercise, that is, the same amount of work, at a lower energy cost. You are

*L*isten to
your body.

more efficient. As a simpler version, you can just record the distance or the time of your stepping activity and then record the perceived exertion or other measure of its intensity of effort.

Non-repetitive, creative aerobic activities

Other types of activities, known as aerobics or aerobic dance, may be more interesting, may challenge the coordination, and may engage more muscle groups than the above cyclic activities. Such creative activities are as effective as cyclic activities, possibly more so. You may enjoy creative activities more and get a total body experience. Women feel more human than robotic. Activities can be less structured and you can avoid any repetitive trauma injury.

With aerobics, you can twist and turn, use all major muscles of your body and enjoy creating a multitude of new and interesting movements. Done to energetic music, you can get quite a workout!

◆ If you have had any dance training, you can freely perform the techniques of modern dance or ballet.

◆ Put on country music or country rock and do line dances.

◆ Practice your footwork for tennis, volleyball, basketball, fencing .

◆ Do the cheerleading drills seen or performed when you were younger.

◆ Use jazz music to dance jazz steps.

◆ Walk, hop, skip, jump, leap, slide, etc. alternating among these.

◆ Dance-walk about the house or a room.

The important thing to remember is to ele-

You can create your own aerobics or join a class.

The important thing to remember is to elevate your heart rate and increase your breathing. You can select a special time to perform aerobics or you can integrate aerobics into your daily activities, such as grocery shopping, cleaning the house, taking care of sleeping children or watching television. You should strive for at least 30 minutes of aerobic activity a day, and try to fit in one 15 minute continuous period.

If you don't have time for 15 minutes, take 5 minutes three times a day. Gradually work up to the longer period which is more effective in causing long-term improvement.

Anaerobics

These are fun to do, but are activities near your maximum predicted heart rate—above your determined effort or target heart rate zone calculated for aerobics. With anaerobics, you experience what is known as oxygen debt, feeling the need for more air, breathing very deeply. Each exercise period is less than 2 minutes, usually 10-20 seconds. You will repeat these 5-20 times. Anaerobic fitness levels are measured with respect to power—amount of work done with respect to time.

Test of anaerobic power

Record the time it takes to run up a flight of stairs as fast as possible. Multiply the height of stairs by your body weight to measure work done. To measure power, divide work done by the time required to run up the stairs.

Check your anaerobic power level weekly.

As with aerobic activities, only your imagination limits the kinds of anaerobic activities in which you can engage. Here are suggestions for anaerobic activities. Select what you like or create your own anaerobic activities.

◆ Run in place as fast as possible for 10 seconds, rest for 20 seconds.

◆ Run up a flight of stairs, descend slowly.

◆ Perform fencing lunges, tennis lunges, volleyball jumps, and blocks/spikes or other sports movements as fast as possible for 10 seconds (use soft surface or well-padded shoes).

◆ Swim the length (or width) of a pool as fast as possible, return with a lazy stroke.

◆ Perform fast dancing for 10 seconds (whatever gets you very tired) and then just move upper body in slow swaying movement for 20 seconds.

◆ Jump rope as fast as possible.

◆ Create your own challenge.

◆ Repeat each of the above 10 times.

Enjoy the sensations of the increased heart rate and elevated breathing rate and deeper air exchange. Let them become a part of your daily life. When you have a choice of walking somewhere or lazily completing the task, run or try to do the task as fast as safely possible—having fun doing it. Do it for yourself.

Self-awareness, self-assessment, self-acceptance

Frequency, number of repetitions, length of time, and intensity are unique for your characteristics.

Be eclectic, determining what is most fun for you on a particular day and time of day. Even if you only walk around in your residence as you prepare the shopping list, the things you need to do that day, or to reduce stress, it feels good to breathe faster and get your blood pumping so you can feel it. Enjoy the throb of your heart.

Chapter Eight

Use the A-B-C's of Woman-Centered Fitness

At the heart of all our healthy, women-centered fitness and quality of life programs is the integrated functioning of our bodies in all types of movement. You could think of this as the underlying A-B-C's of movement.

A is for *agility* and *adaptability*
B is for *balance*
C is for *coordination, creativity* and *control*
S is for *sensory awareness, sports* and *speed*

Along with joint fitness, muscle fitness, and cvr fitness, the A-B-C's form the connection that make our bodies perform. For example, you might exercise on a leg extension weight machine and develop leg strength, but you need more than leg strength to climb stairs. Coordination and balance are the keys to successful stair climbing.

Some A-B-C's activities

◆ Play wall-ball. This game develops your perceptual-motor skills of eye-hand coordination, quickens response and movement time, develops skilled movement patterns. Set a table adjacent a wall and use the table surface and wall surface for your rebounding surfaces. Hit the ball so it will strike the front wall and rebound to the table. You will return the ball to the wall. The wall is your partner! Goals and modifications could be to strike the ball 50 times successively, alternate hitting forehand and backhand, or strike with your non-dominant hand.

◆ Play with a balloon. Hit into the air and keep it there.

◆ Dribble a ball around the house. Use both hands.

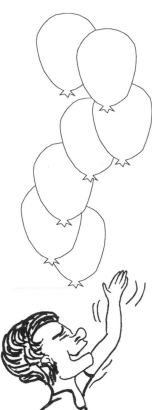

Motion-fit is the result of practicing your A-B-C's.

All the above can be varied by changing the size, color, shape, and texture of the ball or balloon. You can use either or both hands; you also could use your foot or feet. In this case the floor or any wall will be used. If you feel confident of your abilities, invite a friend to join you. Better yet, help her to acquire the A-B-C's too!

Many of the activities described in the previous chapters consisted of one or more components of the A-B-C's of woman-centered fitness. Creative aerobics, movement focus, movement continuity, balance skills, etc. are some examples. In this chapter you will learn how to evaluate and specifically practice A-B-C's.

Adaptability

This is the ability to cope, respond to the unexpected, and function in varying environments with different devices; also using the right and left arms, legs, feet, and hands equally well.

Changing body positions is known as agility and involves sitting, lying, climbing, twisting, turning, somersaulting, rolling, crawling, stooping and changing from one position to another with ease. Don't expect to do all of these equally well, but the ability to change your body positions and head orientation is very important. Blood tends to pool in our feet and legs when we stand for long periods of time. Our systems become sluggish and we do not react efficiently to required tasks. The more we practice agility and adaptability, the more fully alive we will feel.

Adaptability/agility exercise course

Study the instructions below and be sure that you know what is expected to complete the course. Place a timing device at the starting position and stand near the chair. Start the watch as you begin. Perform all exercises at each site as fast as you safely can, moving from one site to the next as quickly as possible. When you return to the end, stop the watch and record your time. Repeat two more times.

+ Start the timing device.
+ Sit and stand 3 times.
+ Walk rapidly to the table and crawl under it from one end to the other.
+ Walk rapidly to the sofa and lie face up.
+ Lift legs above your shoulders and lower them 3 times.
+ Rise from sofa and walk rapidly 10 steps.
+ Sit on floor, turnover, and crawl 6 steps (count each hand movement as a step).
+ Rise and walk rapidly to the bed.
+ Lie on the bed and roll one revolution to the right, then once to the left.
+ Rise, walk rapidly to starting chair, sit, and stop the watch. Record your time.

Shuttle run—exchange shoes

Place a pair of shoes at each end of a room or corridor. (It is recommend that you use an open space with shoes about 15 feet apart, if possible.) Start the timing device, run to the other end of the room, pick up one shoe, and bring it back to the starting point. Pick up a shoe there, carry it to other end, and continue until they have been exchanged with the other pair. Run back to the starting point and stop the watch.

Adaptability/ Agility Course
Score 1_____
Score 2_____
Score 3_____

Shuttle Run
Score 1_____
Score 2_____
Score 3_____

Balance

Balance is the ability to move without falling. There are two types: dynamic and static. You probably do not have difficulty in maintaining your balance when standing, sitting or lying. But what if you put in-line skates on your feet? How well could you balance yourself? Review the balancing activities in Chapter 4 in which you stand on one foot and then on the balls of both feet and on the ball of one foot.

Moving creates new problems. Moving rapidly, walking on an icy sidewalk and trying new activities such as in-line skating, skiing, playing volleyball, and rock climbing often place you at risk of falling. Lack of skill and unfamiliarity with the movement, as well as accelerations, disrupt balance mechanisms. You must adapt. Practice is very important if you are to maintain and improve your balance skills.

Stand on one leg and dress yourself

Every morning use a standing position to put on your underwear, jeans, and shoes etc. This includes standing on one leg while putting on one shoe and tying your shoe laces. Then put on the other shoe.

Walk a line, balance beam, or curb

Practice the following using a line on the floor or a 2" x 4" x 8' piece of lumber. Later you can select balance beams and other "thin lines" for moving.

*C*reate *your own sequence of balancing activities and time your performance.*

- ◆ Walk forward the length of board.
- ◆ Walk backward the length of board.
- ◆ Walk sideboards the length of board.
- ◆ Walk forward to the center and turn 180 degrees and walk backward to the end.

◆ Walk forward to the center and turn 360 degrees and walk forward to the end

◆ Step forward with the right leg and swing the left high enough to cause the heel of right foot to lift from the board prior to placing the left foot on the board. Continue stepping in this manner. until you reach the end of the board.

◆ Check off the activities you can perform and those which you cannot. Practice until all can be achieved. Time yourself on performance of combinations of two or more of these.

Coordination

Coordination is the ability to perform complex movements using more than one body part, as well as to manipulate objects. All our movements require some amount of coordination, but when we practice new and intricate movements we keep our nervous system sharp.

Control is the ability to precisely perform exactly the way you wanted to perform. Putting a golf ball into the cup, shooting a basketball through the hoop, threading a needle, painting a floral scene, drawing a child's face, writing your name and decorating a cake are examples of coordination activities in which near exact control is necessary for success.

There are many common activities that can be used to improve and maintain your coordination and control:

◆ Play scales on a piano.
◆ Speed type on a computer or typewriter.
◆ Learn a folk or a country line dance.
◆ Knit, crochet, do macramé.
◆ Play soccer (or dribble with your feet).
◆ Skip rope.
◆ Play hopscotch.

Coordination/ control exercises should be selected for enjoyment and not just exercise.

* Play jacks.
* Pick up sticks, stack blocks.
* Pound a row of nails into a board.

Trace a star

This is a great activity for developing coordination of both hands. Draw a large star on an 8 1/2 by 11 inch paper. Now draw an identical star on another paper. Start the timer. Trace one star with the right hand as you trace the other star with your left. Repeat in a continuous tracing until you have traced the stars 5 times. Stop the timing device. Record your score as the number of seconds to complete the task, and note which direction you performed the tracing. Check clockwise as cw; counterclockwise as ccw.

Trial 2: Change the direction for each of your two hands.

Trial 3: Use the cw or ccw movement for both hands.

Tracing a Star		
Trial 1 score_____	right cw____ccw____	left cw____ ccw____
Trial 2 score_____	right cw____ccw____	left cw____ ccw____
Trial 3 score_____	right cw____ccw____	left cw____ ccw____

You are the evaluator—if your precision is not satisfactory, the score is not valid. Try again.

Forearm coordination

This activity is modified from AAHPERD Functional Fitness Test. Five markers (coasters or circles made from cardboard) are needed. Place the 5 identical cans (soup, juice, etc.) in front of you. Place markers 12 inches to the left, to the right, in front of, and at 45 degrees to the right and to the left as shown:

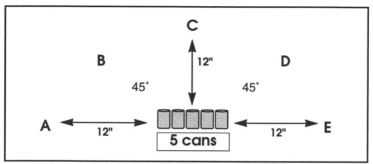

To record your performance and check progress and maintenance of coordination use a timing device to test yourself on how fast you can complete the following actions:

- ◆ Start the timing device.
- ◆ Lift one can and move to A, turning the can over before setting it on the marker.
- ◆ Repeat, placing a can on markers at B, C, D, & E.
- ◆ Reverse the sequence; pick up the last can at E and return to starting position, turning it upright again.
- ◆ Continue with the other 4 cans in order from position E, D, C, B, and A.
- ◆ Stop timer and record elapsed time.
- ◆ Repeat with the other hand.

Can Lift
1 right_____
left_____
2 right_____
left_____
3 right_____
left_____

Creative activities

You can create your own coordination and control activities. Play a cassette tape or CD and move to the music using any combination of coordination patterns. You can choreograph the grapevine pattern, side slides, toe pointing, heel-toe taps, and stomping of country dancing in your own order. Use of ballet, modern dance and folk dance steps can be combined as you wish. You can even have fun mixing in some sports movements, such as fencing advances, retreats and lunges, volleyball jumps, basketball slides and jump-shots, simulated tennis serves and drives, and simulated rope skipping. When you create, you do not assess your performance objectively (such as with a timing device). You will subjectively assess your feeling of how you performed by means of a perceived coordination rating. Perceived coordination ratings are as effective as objective measurements of performance—sometimes actually more effective, since you are evaluating the performance quality directly, instead of evaluating the product of the performance.

Perceived Coordination Rating Scale

5 very easy to do, in balance all the time, body feels great
4 a few problems with balance, but basically easy
3 some difficulty, lost some actions
2 felt clumsy, many balance and coordination problems
1 could not complete the sequence of actions

Control of movements

Objective tests can be devised for you to practice your control of both arms and both legs. Here are some easy ones to construct:

◆ Draw a square. Measure for accuracy (all sides must be equal). Duplicate the exact square in another space on the paper. Duplicate the square with the other hand.

◆ Write your name. Now write your name with your other hand.

◆ Draw a circle in the sand with your foot. Duplicate it elsewhere. Duplicate it with the other foot.

◆ Pour water into a glass, a bottle, and a narrow-necked vase. Pour salt into a salt shaker. Practice frequently to maintain accuracy, precision, and regulation of force.

Sensory awareness

Sensory awareness is the ability to sense where and how we move (kinesthesia), to perceive the movement of objects, and to coordinate our movements to these objects, such as catching a ball or hitting a shuttlecock with a badminton racquet. This ability is also termed perceptual-motor skill. Our ability to respond to the sensory input by means of movement is referred to as speed of response or reaction time.

Can you sense your movements—hear, touch, visualize and feel your movements? Refer to Chapter 4 on how to develop sensory aspects of movement; then try these additional activities.

Develop a sense of oneness with your body and feel the movement.

Imagine and sense these walking actions

◆ Walk naturally.
◆ Walk as if a ghost making no sound.
◆ Stomp like an angry or clumsy giant .
◆ Walk on the balls of your feet as if you were a ballet dancer.

Perform dribbling movements

◆ Dribble a ball as you walk
   –one bounce to each step.
   –two bounces to each step.
   –one bounce to each two steps.
◆ Dribble a ball as you run
   –one bounce to each step.
   –two bounces to each step.
   –one bounce to each two steps.
◆ Repeat using the other hand.

Perform tossing movements

- ◆ Toss a ball up and catch it as you walk
  –one toss and catch each two steps.
  –one toss and catch each step.
- ◆ Toss the ball up and catch it as you run
  –one toss and catch each two steps.
  –one toss and catch each step.
- ◆ Toss the ball and catch it as you lunge
  –one toss and catch on each lunge and
  then return holding ball.
  –one toss and catch on the lunge and
  toss and catch on return.
- ◆ Repeat using other hand and lunging leg.

*L**earn to respond
to movements of
objects and develop
spatial awareness.***

Throw at a wall

- ◆ Throw a ball against a wall and catch it;
continue for 20 catches using one hand.
  - ◆ Use the other hand.
  - ◆ Throw with one hand and catch with the
other.
  - ◆ Time your performances.
  - ◆ Throw and catch with a partner.

Speed of movement and response

This is the ability to respond or react quickly
to a signal, a thrown object, an unexpected
action, or a danger. You can practice this by performing all ball activities with a partner. You also
can play video and arcade games. Creating your
own reaction-time game can be done using a TV
set. Watch TV and respond to each change in
scene as follows: when the scene flashes from a
close-up to another close-up, clap hands above
your head. When a scene flashes from a close-up
to a distance scene, clap hands behind your back.
You can change your movements to any pattern
you like. You can also respond by moving differently whenever speakers change.

Create your own games

It is most important that you create your own games—competitive, noncompetitive, with rules, without rules, change the rules as you play, etc. whatever you wish. You might play variations of volleyball, basketball, tennis, paddle ball, racquet ball, badminton or soccer with two or more players. Scale the area of play to an appropriate size. Serve or start the play any convenient manner you wish. Keep score, or not, as you wish. The object of the games are to enjoy your ability, not to win, but enjoy feeling your body and integrated self as you move in relationship to other women. You will develop spatial awareness of the speed and direction of the movement of the ball and those with whom you are playing. Then you will learn to move quickly to respond to the position of the ball and catch, strike, kick or tap the ball appropriately.

Think of teammates as facilitators to your development of self instead of as opponents.

Games are environment-constrained. Within games and sports, you learn to manipulate and cope with the changing environment. We become more aware of ourselves and others. Awareness of yourself with respect to others is a beautiful feeling and enhances our sharing and challenging of ourselves.

Respect those who play well and aspire to play as well. If you are at a higher level than another woman, play with your racquet/bat/ball in your non-dominant hand. Improve your symmetry. Improve your A-B-C's.

If you are highly skilled, you should be able to place the ball exactly as you wish. For example, hit a tennis ball to the far right baseline, then to the far left baseline, then to the front right, and then to the front left regardless of where you receive the ball. That is skill. The world of sports has become an arena to win the extrinsic reward and to beat the opponents, without thought of developing better skills in each individual. How often, is the point won by the errors of an opponent than by the skill of self?

Think of games to enhance *your* A-B-C's!

Chapter Nine

Inner Strength Through Relaxation

Modern life, with its complexities, pressures of competition, long hours of remaining in one posture at a stressful job and the continual race against time to complete a task often brings excess tension to our bodies. This tension is further intensified by such factors as fears, feelings of inadequacy or insecurity, frustrations, anxieties, and mental or physical fatigue. Thus, we can become a "wired" person, inefficient, aching or feeling tight or generally miserable and ready to "blow-up.' Sleep is not sufficiently long enough or deep enough to reduce the levels of tension created during the day. We say we can't relax; we need to relax; we are so tense!

What is tension?

The term tension designates a general condition of activity throughout the body. It includes the contractions of skeletal and postural muscles, as well as the muscles of our organs, such as the heart, blood vessels, intestines and hormonal glands. The tension in our brain and peripheral nerves are necessary to keep us awake and alert. Optimum tension is used to define this normal baseline of tension optimally produced to meet the needs of our active behavior at any particular instant in time. Optimum tension varies throughout the day, and from day to day. Usually, tension is lowest in the morning. Tension builds as we work, study, socialize, and engage in intense thinking. Tension often drops after a meal. Many of us cannot prevent tension build-up or extraneous tension from affecting out behavior. We cannot release this extra tension.

True relaxation takes you to the bare minimum state of tension necessary to still exist.

Relaxation is nothing more than a release of tension. This means that only the residual tension required to maintain our automatic life processes, such as blood flow, nerve conductivity and respiration, will exist. All extraneous tension, such as muscle contraction in muscles not required to function, is eliminated. Furthermore, the mind itself relaxes and experiences a euphoria.

There are two fundamental processes for relaxing—primary and side-effects. The primary relaxation process is one in which you actively, consciously strive to relax. The side-effects process is just that, a side-effect of relaxation during another activity. Sleep, recreational play, exercise, sports, or other activities can produce side-effects of relaxation. Sleep usually reduces the tension levels, unless you toss and turn or have nightmares as you sleep. Likewise, sports may induce anxiety if competition is too intense. Activities may relax some parts of the body but not others. For example, walking and cycling may be performed with tension in the shoulders or hands as the rest of the body utilizes only enough tension required to run or bike. Recreation, however, does have the potential to enhance relaxation because:

*R*elaxation can be acquired as a side-effect of other activities.

◆ Recreation replaces the tension-causing activity.
◆ Intellectual activity is replaced by physical activity.
◆ Recreation is chosen, not imposed.
◆ Recreation is all consuming and absorbing to the individual.
◆ There is satisfaction in the recreational activity.

Primary relaxation can be acquired, but must be practiced. For those persons who need to learn to relax, that is, persons having high tension levels, relaxation does not come easily. These persons have what might be termed the Neuromuscular Hypertension Syndrome. But it is never too late to learn. You can learn to relax by bringing the following to your practice session:

- ◆ patience
- ◆ attentiveness
- ◆ quiet environment
- ◆ restful position
- ◆ commitment

Practicing relaxation means taking time to relax. You must find time—relaxing does not come naturally—or so it seems in the human world of high level thinking, concern for others, ourselves, and stress from decision-making and response to behavior of others.

Where to practice? You need a quiet space—or maybe one where you can play relaxing music to drown out other distracting sounds and mellow you. Sounds of nature, ocean surf, birds, and classical music are ideal if soft and flowing. Select your music for background appeal only, not for active listening.

T en minutes a day is all you need to practice relaxation.

Darkness is preferred—you can put a blindfold over your eyes. A scarf or a dark-colored piece of cloth over your eyes works great!

Position for relaxing? A lying position is best, though sitting can be utilized. Headstand positions also have been used. Use a soft pad under the body, and place a rolled towel under the knees to reduce stress to the lower back. You might also wish a small pillow or rolled towel under the head. Lie on your back with arms along the side of the body and legs extended and naturally rotating outward. Be comfortable!

How to relax?

Relaxation methods have been practiced as long as recorded history. The many religious recluses and monks used concentration practices to establish a certain relaxed state of mind. Buddhism, Zen, and Yoga have relaxation as an integral part of their philosophy of life. Hypnosis was used by nomads to endure long treks through the desert and by Tibetan tribes needing to survive in very cold climates. Entertainers have combated "stage fright" by lying and simulating death prior to going on the stage.

Different forms of relaxation work for different persons, and sometimes one method may work better at different stress levels. There are two categories of relaxation approaches: *tension control* and *auto-suggestion* (or *hypnosis/ imagery)*. Both forms have been modified in many ways by many clinical psychiatrists, sports psychologists, relaxation experts, therapists, and others teaching and researching relaxation techniques. All approaches have potential merit. Choose one or a combination of these for yourself. Three approaches will be described in the following sections as practical, effective and easy to learn.

Tension control—the Jacobson technique

Tension control is more than relaxation, it is the ability to recognize and regulate the optimal tension for a given situation. This is considered to be a muscular approach. You concentrate on evaluating the level of tension in each muscle group and learn to recognize levels of tension, especially unwanted levels. Jacobson assumed that eliminating muscle tension would induce mental relaxation as a by-product.

How it works

Initially, to learn to feel muscle tension you may want a friend to provide resistance to movement. For example, try to flex the forearm (contracting the biceps bracchi muscle) and your friend will hold the forearm immobile.

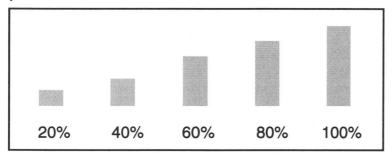

Contract maximally for less than a second. Then relax the muscle as completely as possible.

Next contract 50% of maximum for less than a second. Relax as completely as possible.

P̄ractice regulating muscle tension.

Repeat several times and then try different increments: zero, 10%, 20%, 30%, etc. until you think you can control the tension levels.

Sequence order: left biceps, left triceps, left hand flexors, left hand extensors, repeat with right; left foot flexors, left foot extensors, left leg flexors, left leg extensors, left thigh flexors, left thigh extensors, repeat with right; abdominal muscles, respiratory muscles, shoulder area, upper back, neck, face.

When practicing alone you can move the body part as you contract the muscle. Later you can perform without movement, merely thinking the muscle to contract. Next use decrements from maximum contraction to zero for each muscle. At the end, all muscles should be relaxed and you should feel devoid of tension. Most important, you have learned to recognize early signs of unwanted tension and to control tension levels in your muscles.

Auto-suggestion—the Schultz technique

Mental relaxation is your goal, and muscle relaxation is merely the means by which you attain this goal. Since self-suggestion is a part of life, you can invoke a suggestion of a feeling, awareness, or image into the relaxation situation. Schultz used the terms "heaviness and warmth" to transfer the excitation state of mind to a relaxed and mental quiet state.

In your lying environment, imagine your muscles as being heavy and getting warm. Concentrate on feeling these characteristics. When this has been satisfactorily achieved, think of the vascular system and think of the blood flow as being sluggish and warm. The first trials will not be as heavy and warm a feeling as later practice trials, but this is O.K.

Slowly stretch after the practice session to bring yourself back to reality.

Schada's method

The approaches of Jacobson and Schultz were studied and modified by Schada to produce a very effective relaxation technique based upon breathing practices. This also is an auto-suggestive body-focused approach

Lengthening of exhalation can be a "quick fix" relaxation.

Background music and the voice of a relaxation teacher may help you to relax more quickly than practicing alone. You may, however, feel intimidated or distracted by either the teacher or the music. Therefore, you need not use either. The following guidelines are all that are needed to achieve relaxation.

The *environment* is one in which all sensory stimuli are eliminated or reduced. All music and talking from the teacher is low-keyed and a constant monotonous background droning. These sounds are not concentrated upon but merely heard.

The *position* is a supine position (lying on your back) with cushioning, such as a mat, under the body and pillows or other supports placed at possible stress sites. Support under the knees releases strain on the lower back and at the knees. Support under the arms releases strain at the elbows. You may wish a support under the head. The arms are at the side, slightly flexed and palms down. In this position no muscular contraction is required; the body has given in to gravity. Clothing is loose fitting, glasses are removed and eyes are closed.

Practice 1 Attend to your breathing. Breathe naturally and easily noting your exhalation and inhalation. In your mind's eye see and feel the rise and fall of the abdomen and the chest. Observe, in your mind, the phenomenon of natural, involuntary breathing.

Breathing improves relaxation; relaxation improves breathing.

Practice 2 Begin as with practice 1. Lengthen the exhalation of your breathing, Give in to the exhalation without lengthening the inhalation. Conjure images of your chest being loose, collapsing, or rising and slowly falling. Feel a pause after the exhalation as the body prepares to inhale.

Practice 3 Begin as with practice 2. This is the first of a series of conscious or volitional muscular release practices. The preferred arm is the site of attention. Continue to breath and use imagery on the exhalation to think relaxation of the arm. You can use mental pictures of heavy arm, floating arm, arm through the mat or other visions of the arm. Terminate the practice with stretching, sit up and stretch again, and restore your alertness.

Practice 4 Begin as with practice 3. Continue the series of body segment, conscious muscular release practices. When relaxation has been achieved with one body segment, continue with the next using appropriate imagery:

Segment	Image
both arms	heavy, sinking sensation
shoulder girdle	of flattening, looseness and dropping backward
neck	heavy, being pulled apart
upper body	a sack, see yourself
both legs	falling, heavy, sinking
lower back	sinking self connected
face	eye brows, jaw, mouth, hollowness, openness
total self	floating on a cloud, see self from outside

Stretch at end of each session. Remain at one practice focus for several days or until success is attained. Twitching signifies muscle tension letting go.

Use of other suggestive images

Think of an external image, i.e., a pleasant ocean scene or a sky of fireworks. Concentrating on self-imposed images other than the self/body is a viable alternative to body-focused techniques. All are some form of imagery and can be used to induce relaxation. Guard against concentrating on the external image so much that you begin to fantasize and dream of actions that excite you and inhibit total relaxation. The use of imaging may be one of the easiest ways for you to promote a reduced tension level.

Body-focused imagery is one of the easiest and deepest ways to relax.

The essence of relaxation

No matter which method of relaxation you choose, the goal is the same: *to relax.* This means that you will forget the world, its stresses and all its distractions. Your body will belong to you. Through relaxation you will be able to further your pursuit of self-awareness and self-acceptance.

All three methods, *Jacobson, Schultz,* and *Schada* have proven effective for women. Personally, I know that the Schada method can induce relaxation to the degree that you can "go outside your body." That is a beautiful, peaceful phenomenon! In order to achieve this you must practice, be patient, attentive, and committed. This requires total release of the brain and its thought processes.

Plan to relax, relax, relax each day.

As previously mentioned, there are many approaches to relaxation. Yoga, with its asanas (postures) and breathing exercises, can easily be included in your relaxation program. Zen meditation and other Eastern-based, movement focused, and other quiet activities are effective ways to produce relaxation.

Chapter Ten

Eat to Become

We all engage in eating—it is a requisite to survival. The important issue is whether or not our eating behavior facilitates our well-being, mitigates against it, or is not really a factor. If we have a stable weight and do not fluctuate up and down dramatically, obviously our eating behavior matches our lifestyle and thus corresponds with our approved state-of-being. If we eat too little or too much and show dramatic decreases or increases in body weight and energy level, we have inadequate, and possibly dangerous, nutrition. If you became familiar with your body as suggested in chapter 1, you will already have become aware of your body weight. Remember the importance of self-awareness, including nutritional self-awareness and the effects upon our body weight, lifestyle, and well-being. This is necessary in the process of acquiring sound nutritional habits.

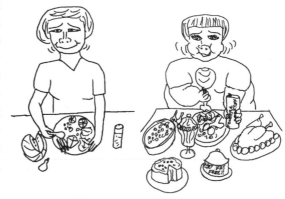

Eat to live, don't live to eat!

Nutrients

Nutrients are substances that nourish or promote growth and repair the natural wastage of our organic life. We need six basic groups of nutrients: water, carbohydrates, fats, proteins, vitamins, minerals. The carbohydrates, fats, and proteins are measured and analyzed according to the number of calories they contain. Calories are equivalent to the energy that our

Water balance is essential both inside and outside our body cells.

bodies can use or can store as fat from the foods we eat. On the average, women eat, and need, 2000 calories a day. It is your lifestyle and genetics that will determine whether or not you need less than, or more than, this amount.

Water—the most essential nutrient! We realize the absence of water soonest and its absence is fatal more quickly than absence of the other nutrients. Since nutrition is not merely eating, but consists of the processes whereby the body utilizes the ingested food, water is vital to nutrition. Water (including that in our blood) transports nutrients to cells of the body and waste products and other substances away from the body. Our body is 70% water.

Carbohydrates—one of the major fuel sources or suppliers of energy to the body. These are the sole suppliers of energy to the brain and central nervous system and also are necessary for the metabolism of selected other nutrients. The three types of carbohydrates are mono-, di- and poly-saccharides according to their complexity. The most complex are also termed starches and require more time and processing to break them down to the basic energy source called glucose. These polysaccharides also contain fiber, minerals, vitamins and even proteins.

Fats—essential, believe it or not! Fats are composed of oils and are classified in a number of ways, such as high and low density lipids or mono- or poly- unsaturated and saturated fats. Some fat foods, such as butter, margarine, bacon, and salad oils are readily identifiable as fats. Others, such as cheese, milk, eggs and nuts are not so recognizable. Although the average woman in the United States eats 40% or more calories of fat in her diet, not all fats are detrimental to her health. Beneficial functions of fats are those serving as carriers of the fat-soluble vitamins A, D, E, and K. Fats stored beneath the skin protect the body from heat loss. Fat also protects the body from injury. Fats are essential to healthy skin and normal growth. Fats are a more concentrated source of energy than carbohydrates, yielding more than twice the number of calories per unit of weight.

Cholesterol—a waxy substance produced by fats and by the body to form membranes around cells, has been suggested as a contributor to coronary heart disease. If excess saturated fats are ingested, the cholesterol can clog the arteries as it is transported by the low density fats in the blood. High density fats (HDL) appear to be able to transport the cholesterol without clogging the arteries and can absorb cholesterol. Cholesterol can be converted into vitamin D when touched by sunlight or ultraviolet light. Cholesterol aids in metabolism of carbohydrates, is the main supplier of the essential adrenal steroid hormones and exists throughout the body organs and tissues.

Eat 3 HDL for every LDL.

Proteins—the body builders. Except for water, the largest amount of material in our body is protein, the builder and repairer of tissues. Protein also combines with iron to form hemoglobin in the blood. In addition, protein is used to manufacture hormones and enzymes. The building of antibodies to fight infections also is facilitated by proteins.

There are complete proteins and incomplete proteins. The complete ones, found in animal sources, contain all of the 8 essential amino acids required for maintenance of health. Yogurt is considered an ideal protein food substitute for meat. Women eating a fruit and vegetable diet often do not get enough of the essential amino acids. Conversely, however, most women and men, in the United States are apt to eat 2 to 3 times more protein than necessary.

Vitamins—silent helpers. These organic substances are essential to the proper functioning of our bodies since they act as catalysts in metabolic function. Most vitamins cannot be manufactured or synthesized by human beings, but must be obtained through foods. All essential vitamins (A, C, D, E, K, and B series 1, 2, 6, 12, 15) can easily be obtained through leafy green vegetables, milk and grains. Vitamins are not miracle workers, but lack of them can create such problems as anemia, fatigue, bone, teeth, joint and vascular problems, and blood clotting. Adequate ingestion of vitamin sources will prevent and reverse such conditions. Thus, vitamins are thought to be miracle workers. For example, brussels sprouts, cauliflower, broccoli and cabbage block the conversion of cancer-producing chemicals to active cancer because of their vitamins and minerals.

Minerals—essentials! There are 18 minerals required for body maintenance, but only six have been identified on the RDA tables (Recommended Daily Allowances). Men and women require similar amounts of phosphorus and iodine. Men require higher intakes of magnesium and zinc, whereas women require more calcium and iron. Women often do not obtain enough calcium or iron and thus are at risk to acquire osteoporosis and anemia, respectively. Best sources of calcium are milk, cheese, yogurt, tofu, sardines and green,leafy vegetables. Best sources for iron are meats, fish, poultry, legumes; green leafy vegetables and whole and enriched grains. Salt and potassium (bananas) also should be included in your diet.

Beta carotenes and bioflavoids are essentials.

You need to eat foods rich in calcium and iron.

Hunger and eating habits

One problem with nutrition is that we often choose to eat or not to eat because of feelings of depression, anger, anxiety, nervousness, fear, boredom, frustration, etc., rather than because of our physiological state of hunger. We often eat or employ other mal-adaptive eating behavior when we fail to develop appropriate coping skills to life. Such eating behaviors are triggered by false hunger signals. It is important to become aware of your state of hunger. We erase the dichotomies again and draw *hunger* on a continuum circle leading from no hunger to over hunger and back to no hunger. You should always try to eat before over hunger occurs, since this stage includes weakness, nausea, headaches, and dangers to one's health. At various places along the circle is false or pseudo hunger. Strategies must be formulated to avoid eating during false hunger. These are presented later. Let's look at balanced nutrition first.

*E*at whenever you are hungry is sound advice, but learn to recognize false hunger signals.

Balanced nutrition

Although we have marvelous abilities to adapt to adverse nutritional habits and short-term deficits, many times it seems as though we push this adaptability to extremes. Sometimes our bodies are not able to cope or adapt, whether because of frequency or duration of misuse or because of unexpected or periodic changes in the physiology of the body. Such changes include menstruation, menopause, fevers, other illnesses, and diseases. Through our experience we have found that balanced nutrition and adequate exercise are essential to our sense of daily well-being. Daily well-being is defined as sufficient energy and movement skills to easily perform daily living tasks. Guidelines for acquiring balanced nutrition have been published by the United States Department of Agriculture), These guidelines are based upon current knowledge and calculated averages. Knowing and following the USDA pyramid of foods is sound advice.

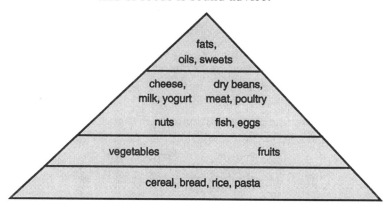

Study the four levels of the pyramid, starting at the foundation. Bread, cereal, rice, and pasta constitute a necessary group of foods, since they are high in minerals such as iron, and are carbohydrates which provide the energy for daily activities. The next level, equally important, are the fruit and vegetable groups. These foods are rich in vitamins and low in calories. They also are primarily carbohydrates. Some food nutrition experts think this level should be the foundation of the pyramid.

On the next level are the proteins, vitamins, group of dairy products (milk, yogurt and cheese) and meat, poultry, fish, dry beans, eggs, and nuts. Growing children need more of this group than adults; again, this is an essential part of the pyramid. Milk is still the best single source of Vitamin D. There now is a no-fat milk that tastes the same as 2% because cellulose has been added. Women who cannot ingest milk can substitute yogurt, lactose-reduced or acidophilis milk.

The peak of the pyramid is often termed the "culprit" or "undesirable" part, but this is not the case. Fats, oils and sweets are essential to the diet. It is the overeating of this group combined with the undereating of the other groups that result in problems. Many times this top level group can be derived from the other levels of the pyramid, such as sugars of fruits that are sweets. But the fact remains, less of this group is required than those foods listed at the other levels. Balance means some of all, more of the lower levels.

Eating strategies I: What we eat

Here are some specific eating guidelines concerning the major foods, fats, proteins, and carbohydrates and vitamins and minerals:

◆ Eat lots of fruits and vegetables. Many vitamins are acquired with few calories. Some vegetables have zero calories.

◆ Eat approximately 20% of your foods from fat sources. Fat adds zest to the meal, satiates the hunger feeling, is essential to the body and can be burned during aerobic activity. Fats are best obtained from butter, vegetable oils, olives, avocados, bacon, cheeses, milk, cream, and nuts. Some fats are better than others— mono or low-saturated fats (e.g. avocados and olives) are more easily digested than high-saturated fats. The body requires cholesterol, and genetically, each person has a different level not necessarily based upon what is eaten, but how it

Variety in foods usually results in balanced nutrition.

is utilized. Cholesterol is considered a secondary culprit in cardiovascular-related problems, such as arteriosclerosis. This means, that their appears to be a relationship between the two, but not a cause and effect relationship. Folic acid may be a deterrent to heart problems.

◆ Eat approximately 65% of your foods from carbohydrate sources. These are simple sources for producing energy to move and survive. Breads and grains, pastas, corn, beans, potatoes and rice are examples. One serving of grains may contain as much as 50% of your daily requirements of iron.

◆ Eat approximately 15% of your foods from protein sources (growing children require a greater percent). Beans, peanut butter, nuts, fish, sea food, meats, eggs and cheese are your sources here.

◆ Drink plenty of liquids—water is vital for the body. We can live (survive) a longer period of time without food than we can without water.

Water is essential to life and to effectively utilize foods you eat.

Eating strategies II: When, where, why, & how

When we eat, where we eat, why we eat and how we eat can be strategically planned. Here are some suggestions:

◆ Eat slowly, chewing and savoring the food in your mouth.

◆ Eat in a pleasant environment in order to enjoy your food.

◆ Eat with another person to release mental stress and relax. This may be very soothing to your health.

◆ If you get hungry during the day, eat. If, however, you are always hungry, try to eat only 5 times a day.

◆ Enjoy each moment of the day, whether it be work, leisure activities, relaxation, meditation, telephoning a friend, so you have no time to indulge in eating excess calories.

◆ Identify the factors that trigger false hunger. When triggered, create a diversion using movement, such as flexibility activities of chapter 5, aerobics of chapter 7 etc., to test if hunger is true or false.

◆ Have lowfat, high energy munchies for fillers. Unbuttered popcorn, fruits, vegetables, pretzels, and cereals will fill the void without many calories. Women with high metabolism, burning and needing many calories, can eat such munchies during the day.

Cucumbers, raw or dill-pickled, contain zero calories!

◆ Drink water, or other liquids, such as juices (full strength or watered down) when you feel the urge to eat too soon after having eaten a meal. You know that you can't really be hungry!

◆ Eat raw, steamed, braised, or stir-fryed foods to retain nutrients.

◆ Read the labels on packaged foods but don't become obsessed with labels. Words may be misleading. "Natural" does not mean best! One lite-identified product may not mean less fat than another brand not identified as lite. It is important that you enjoy food, but also consider the ingredients. For example, can microwave popcorn have a "great taste" but be low in fat? Yes, this has been achieved!

◆ Read nutrition literature or new findings in newspapers and magazines. Browse through your libraries and magazine/bookstores. Some magazines give up-to-date reporting of latest nutrition research and excellent nutrition tips. Remember, though, scrutinize what you read. Don't believe everything in print.

When is fat too fat? When is thin too thin?

When fat interferes with your ability to move with ease, fat is too fat. When lack of fat (thinness) interferes with your energy, thin is too thin. In the United States, women have problems associated with being too thin, as well as being too fat.

Reduction of body fat is more effectively done through exercise than through restrictions in the amount of food you eat. Some fat in your body is essential for health, and especially essential if you are pregnant or stricken with an illness. Too little fat in your diet is dangerous. Each of us has a genetic code which predisposes us to a range of thinness or fatness. For example, the size and number of adipocytes (cells which store fat in the form of esterified fatty acids) within our body determine the quantity of fat we will have. Researchers have found that obese persons have three times more adipocytes than non-obese people. Although the number of adipocytes within each person's body appears to be stable, that is, difficult or impossible to change, the size of these cells can be changed. Overeating increases the size of these cells. Starvation reduces the size. In all cases the number of fat cells essentially remains constant. Thus, some women will naturally have more fat, and have a plumper body than others. It is not the amount of fat that is the major problem, but the why of the amount that must be considered.

Whatever your body wight problems, eat a well-balanced diet and MOVE!

To diet or not to diet?

Diet programs often deprive you, causing the inner psychological you not to adapt. Increase your movement duration, intensity, and frequency. Eat a variety of foods and keep the taste of fat—though it can be reduced without feeling deprived. Above all, eat carbohydrates so that the body does not start to use the protein as a substitute for lack of food because of dieting. Protein loss causes loss of muscle tissue.

Tell-tale signs of extra fat

◆ Thighs touch along their entire length.

◆ Abdominal bulge.

◆ Layers of fat under (or a double) chin.

◆ Flab hangs from the upper arm when you lift that arm to shoulder height or higher.

◆ More than an inch of flesh when you grasp a fold of skin at the abdomen, lateral waist, or inner thigh.

If you noticed any of these tell-tale signs, evaluate their effect upon your functionability. Answer the following questions:

◆ Can you tie your shoes sitting in a chair with your feet on the floor?

◆ Can you walk without lateral sway and with your feet facing forward?

◆ Can you easily get into and out of an automobile?

◆ Do you tire with the slightest above-average exertion?

◆ Do you have trouble moving your body?

If you said yes to any of these questions, it might be that you are carrying nonessential fat. Again, only you can answer whether or not this is acceptable for you. Do you want to move with greater ease; be less constrained as to what you could attempt to try; feel the joy of being able to move your body whenever and however opportunities arise? Change your thinking concerning body weight. Think of your ability to move and function with ease and joy, not of how much you weigh.

Too little or too much fat is not the problem—finding the cause is.

Tell-tale signs of too little fat

♦ Can you see the shapes of your bones, especially the ribs and hip bones?

♦ Does your skin appear to be "pasted" on your body?

♦ Are you always tired?

Sound familiar? You probably need to eat more, sleep more, and move in relaxing ways.

What you eat should equal what you burn

Did you know that you could easily burn 5-10 calories a minute? For example, if you run a mile in 12 minutes, you could burn 500 calories. Caloric cost changes from less than 100 when quietly sitting to seven times that when performing very strenuous activity, such as sprinting. If you merely do light physical activity, such as cleaning apartments for eight hours, you could easily burn 2000 calories. If you mix light activity with strenuous activity, you need not be active 8 hours.

Calories Burned Per Hour				
90	250	390	600	800
sit	easy	moderate	somewhat strenuous	very strenuous
Types of Activities				

These are estimates and will differ from yours. Weight, percent of muscle relative to fat, and skill in performing activities will influence the amount of calories burned. Nevertheless, the more intense the activity, the greater the amount of calories consumed. Use the perceived exertion rating concept to estimate calories burned.

Food affects our emotions

We are what we eat is true not only structurally but emotionally. Our body is composed of chemicals; our brain and nervous system function via a communication system dependent upon electric charges and chemical reactions. At every synapse, where one neuron meets another, there are neural transmitters composed primarily of amino acids (the building blocks of protein). It is here that transmission of signals occurs. Thus what we eat will affect how our nervous system transmits signals from place to place. Nicotine (from smoking or inhaling nicotine-saturated air) and alcohol may adversely affect these processes.

Some foods appear to soothe; others bring out aggression. Refined sugar desserts and snacks may provide a pleasurable feeling when eating, but we will most likely experience a loss of energy and some depression a few hours later. Coffee and other drinks with a high content of caffeine also produce these effects. In addition, irritability, sleeplessness, and hypertension are apt to occur.

*E**at foods that energize you.*

Breads and pastas appear to sooth the brain and self. Turkey has been identified as a soothing meat. Herbal use in place of (or in addition to) salt can stabilize and enhance your mood.

Foods you like and how they affect you

Keep a log of the foods that seem to produce undesirable mood shifts. Record the types of cravings you have for foods. Be aware of how foods affect you. Then you will be able to cope with any adverse effects!

Food	Depressed	Energized	Irritable	Other
coffee		✓	✓	
oysters				✓
chocolate	✓	✓		

Food	Depressed	Energized	Irritable	Other

Exercise and nutrition

♦ Aerobic exercise is the best activity to burn fats.

♦ Strength exercises, such as weight lifting, result in weight gain (muscle weighs more than fat). You can tone and change the shape and size of your body without losing weight.

♦ Evaluate new products, "quick-fix" foods, supplements, balanced vitamin tablets, etc. Determine if they are "quack" products or of value to your health. If your diet is a balanced one, you shouldn't need these products.

♦ Obtain medical/nutritional aid if you have a pathological condition.

♦ Evaluate how you feel. Listen to your body to determine the calories and foods you need. Exercise and nutrition are an integrated plan for well-being.

Chapter Eleven

Be Yourself

As you have read throughout this book, YOU, the woman, are the most important element in developing your women-centered fitness, health, enhanced movement lifestyle. *You* decide, *you* assess, *you* become the you want to be.

No one else has the power or the right to tell you what you must think or desire. Everyone may be quick to provide guidelines, suggestions, and inducements for you to act in certain ways, but only you can make the final decision.

Societal norms are not necessarily your norms. These societal norms are guidelines for you. If you fit the norm, then you can use the many suggestions to achieve them.

Obstacles to self-enhancement

There are many obstacles to your finding yourself and accepting your uniqueness. Some of these obstacles and how to cope with them appear below:

This is a high-tech world, with time and labor-saving devices facilitating a sedentary lifestyle. We use machines to clean house, mow the lawn, lift and transport cargo, and generally "replace" our bodies.

What to do

Walk stairs, repeat several times all behaviors that are required only once (sit and stand, reach for a cup, open a drawer), carry and lift weights, park your car at the far end of parking lot, and try to use five minutes of every hour to move.

There is no daily requirement for deep breathing. Most of the time 20% of the air is never moved out of the deep recesses of our lungs. Our lungs and cardiovascular-respiratory system have become sluggish. Some lung problems are primarily due to lack of use of muscles which activate lung expansion.

What to do

Perform breathing exercises. To move the air deep in the lungs, you must practice breathing deeply or engage in strenuous physical activity, such as basketball and distance running, which induces deep breathing. Deep breathing means that you initially emphasize or exaggerate the exhalation. Feel the "blowing out" as a pushing of all the air from the lungs. Later the inhalation can be emphasized, and then both inhalation and exhalation can be lengthened. Practice in the following manner:

+ Inhale and exhale naturally three times.
+ Forcefully lengthen the exhalation to make it last as long as you can.
+ Inhale and exhale naturally five or more times.
+ Forcefully exhale again.
+ Repeat a few more times.
+ Repeat every day, several times a day if you feel that you need more practice.

In the same manner as above, emphasize forced/deep inhalations. Next, perform one-to-three deep inhalation/exhalation cycles followed by natural breathing until you feel comfortable to again repeat the deep breathing cycle.

Leisure is non-existent. Financially too many of us are living in poverty. Family, dependent parent and/or children, job(s), and housekeeping seem to consume all our time.

What to do

Whenever you move, consciously and actively enjoy your movement and feel your body's movement. Walk briskly or jog as you complete your activities of daily living. Do iso-metrics as you sit on the job. Find five minute periods to hit a balloon in the air, dribble a ball, run in place, dance, simulate playing a sport, or simply move your body every direction and manner it can move.

Stress is everywhere: deadlines, others demanding your time and help, not enough time or money, decisions to be made, and hav-ing to cope with many unexpected, traumatic events.

What to do

Spend more time in the shower or bathtub massaging and touching your body, healing it and thereby healing the mind. Take time to walk; concentrate on walking. Observe your environ-ment—hear the birds, see the leaves of the trees, smell the flowers. Engage in relaxation practice. Ask a friend to massage your feet, your shoulders, and any other tense body parts.

Your social life space and subcultures are sedentary.

What to do

Analyze your life spaces and the subcultures to which you belong. You may belong to some of the following—athlete, university student, house-wife, telephone line repair person, country club golfer, mother, lesbian, daughter, teacher, Jewish woman, Feminist Majority member, African American business woman, grandmother, etc. The list is endless. Unfortunately, often with respect to society, and sometimes ourselves, we become a stereotype and define ourselves by our roles. We must avoid stereotyping ourselves. We are dynamic, moving women with unique characteristics. We need to develop support groups which will help us to enhance our lifestyle.

***B**uild a support system for moving.*

Suggest more active activities to enjoy with your friends. Most of our daily living activities require less than 20% of our abilities. We can change that. We have the power to do so. Think of ways to become more diverse in movement. Integrate multicultural movement patterns into your life, i.e., cha cha, t'ai chi, hula dancing. Learn to understand the diversity of others.

***L**earn to play again.*

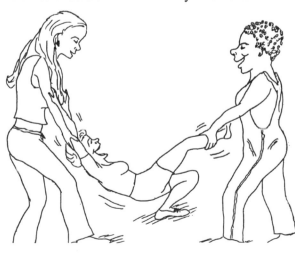

Ideas for integrated movement

Throughout this book you've read descriptions of many ways to move and learn to know and enjoy your body. Now you can combine all the ideas and actions into integrated movements which flow from one concept to another—flexible movements, aerobic-type movements, exploration of qualities of movement, agile movements, etc. You create a movement experience for your pleasure lasting a few minutes or a complete CD.

You may modify the following basic integrated movement ideas or use as they are described. You may move without any musical accompaniment or use music to your liking. However you move, think of the movement as being the focus of your experience and nothing else!

General actions

In this sequence the movements are those used in daily living activities. In some instances you are asked to simulate actions, that is, pretend you are performing the act. You may modify your actions to have fun with the movement. Do each action approximately 30 seconds or repeat the sequence several times.

◆ Walk naturally, walk as slowly as possible, walk using as long a step as possible, walk in a curved path, reverse direction and turn.

◆ March swinging the arms vigorously.

◆ Sit on a chair, stand, walk, sit on the floor.

◆ Simulate reaching and lowering items from shelves and counters; do so using different patterns pretending the items are heavy, then cumbersome, and then light weight.

*U*se daily living *activities for your movement exercise.*

♦ Pretend you are dressing yourself in a standing position.

♦ Simulate swatting flies or mosquitoes.

♦ Simulate painting the ceiling, the wall and the floor.

♦ Repeat the painting action with the other hand.

♦ Simulate playing a musical instrument.

Sports actions

♦ Jog using straight line, curves, and reversals.

♦ Jump simulating basketball shooting, volleyball spikes, etc.

♦ Slide right and left.

♦ Simulate swimming strokes varying the intensity, such as a slow lazy crawl or a competitive backstroke.

♦ Run forward and backward 3 steps.

♦ Simulate tennis strokes.

♦ Create a rhythmic gymnastics routine—use a ball, hoop, streamer.

♦ Simulate a game of racquetball.

♦ Simulate body actions of skiing a slalom course.

♦ Simulate lifting weights varying the action by pretending the weights are light-to-heavy.

Quality of movement

♦ Simulate picking fruit from a tree and vary the ROM and quality of movement, i.e., very fast, very short reaches; slow, long reaching action, reaching in every possible direction.

♦ Simulate a variety of dances: perform a line dance and then vary it with respect to

S̅imulate movements of sport and dance.

ROM, use of arms, forcefulness, and attitude; perform a waltz, square dance, belly dance, ballet dance, etc.

Remember the 3 A's

If you are going to be in control of your development, you need to constantly employ the 3 A's. Always be aware of how your body is moving, how you feel, how you interact with the environment. Attempt to do some appraisal of your movements. These can be qualitative or quantitative, as with timing the speed at which you perform. Change what can be changed if desired. But ultimately, accept how you move and what you can do. With self-acceptance stress is reduced and movement is enhanced.

Our bodies are not merely vehicles with which we get from place-to-place, but they are us—our feelings and avenue by which we sense and interact with our world. We have the potential for doing so much more than we normally attempt.

Self-awareness   *Self-assessment*   *Self-acceptance*

To move is to live

I am, you are, we are moving; you are unique, I am unique; we can move together and separately.

Movement is the essence of a women-centered lifestyle enhancement. Be yourself as you move. Remember your movement is all yours; you need never imitate someone else's movement except for your own wishes. Maximize the benefits of movement by remembering the following:

- Concentrate on the movement.
- Enjoy the movement as an end in itself.
- Move all your body parts.
- Move in all directions and patterns in space.
- Move with varying intensities—light, swinging, free flowing, forceful, etc.
- Move with different attitudes, feelings and focus.
- Move, move, move!

Push yourself to your limit and become the woman you love!

Order Form

Women in Motion

Soft cover edition $11.95 each   no.copies _____
          ISBN 1-884724-03-5

Hard cover edition $18.95 each   no.copies _____
          ISBN 1-884724-04-3

Total enclosed $ _____

Payable to Women of Diversity Productions Inc.
     400 Antique Bay Street
     Las Vegas, NV 89128

Please print clearly to ensure proper delivery.

Name _____

Address _____

City _____State ____ Zip _____

Marlene Adrian, D.P.E., is Professor Emerita at the University of Illinois, Urbana-Champaign, and has conducted numerous workshops in the areas of fitness, movement improvement, self-assessment, sports, and issues relative to biomechanics, safety, aging, and women. She has produced videos and written numerous articles, chapters, and books, including co-authoring *The Complete Encyclopedia of Aerobics and Lifetime Fitness.*

Marlene has conducted extensive biomechanics research relative to walking, footwear, safety in sports, sports and fitness equipment, and she has served on the United States Olympic Sports Equipment and Technology Committee.

A former multi-sports competitor and coach, Marlene was a member of the United States National Women's Epee Fencing team and an international competitor in that sport. She also has been the United States National Women's Sabre Champion.

Currently she is president of Women of Diversity Productions, Inc. is a member of the advisory board of Shape Magazine, and has written articles in this and other fitness magazines.

Acclaimed the Amateur Woman Athlete of the Year by the Wall Street Journal in 1989, Marlene continues to give movement workshops, and participates in hiking, canoeing, tennis, dancing, and fencing. She never passes up a chance to try any physical activity, having built her own house, constructed hiking trails, built fences, remodeled houses, and planted hundreds of trees.

Eliane Mauerberg-deCastro, Sc.D., teaches and conducts research in her native country of Brazil at the State University of São Paulo at Rio Claro. She specializes in the fields of physical activity and disabilities, perception and action, and motor behavior. Eliane spent the last year as a visiting researcher at Indiana University, Bloomington, Indiana. During this time she also conducted workshops in Brazilian dance at several women's music festivals, as well as illustrating this book.

Eliane is an avid sportswoman and has competed in judo, fencing, team handball, and volleyball. She has taught jazz dance and special dance to the deaf and mentally retarded, and continues to coordinate programs of physical activity for disabled groups at her university.

Women of Diversity Productions Inc. is a nonprofit, tax exempt corporation dedicated to the production and dissemination of educational and literary materials and information relative to women's issues, discrimination and alternative thinking.